HUSSAR

In the 15th century, King Matthias of Hungary ordered one out of every twenty houses in a village to provide his fighting forces with one horse soldier. In Hungarian, or Magyar, "husz" means twenty. Such a light cavalryman then came to be known as a "one in 20" - a Hussar.

Hussars wore bright, colorful uniforms and reached their peak of efficiency under Napoleon. They were the elite of his cavalry and were famous for their bold and reckless manner of fighting. Shortly after World War I the Hussars became obsolete.

Library of Congress Cataloging in Publication Data

Boyle, Charles A.   1930 –

      The Black Hussars
      Includes Index
      1.   History 2. Law Enforcement 1. Title

Illustrated

Cover design by Sheila Dufford

Copyright 1999 by Charles A. Boyle
All Rights Reserved
Published by Mabo Publishers, Bellevue, WA
Manufactured in the United States by Bookcrafters, Chelsea, MI

ISBN: 0-9673341-0-1

For Trooper Curt G. Boyle
Washington State Patrol

and his siblings – Andrea, Patrick, Chrissy and,
of course, for Irene

to Karin

ACKNOWLEDGEMENTS

My gratitude to Gregg C. MacDonald. He made this project possible, not only by his encouragement, but in so many other ways. Thanks also to the Duffords – Sheila and Wick; to Sheila for working on the computers, and to Wick for being such a good tennis partner and graciously allowing me to monopolize Sheila's time. I am indebted to Alex Keenan of Applied Arts Publishers in Lebanon, PA for supplying me with the wonderful pictures in Louis Poliniak's book, when *Coal Was King,* and to Bruce Wissinger of the *Johnstown Tribune Democrat* for giving "uncle" Bob Sefick important material that I needed. And finally, my gratitude to the staff at the Cambria County Library for not only their assistance, but for putting up with me during many hours over many days.

THE BLACK HUSSARS

CONTENTS

AUTHOR'S NOTE

From the very beginning of this enterprise I determined that this should not become a schematic, proceeding step by step, year by year, to trace the history of *The Black Hussars* up to the present time. The story is not one of strict chronological order, and the unity I have strived to obtain, whether I have achieved it or not, is one of effect. I have taken up various aspects of the Pennsylvania State Police in their very early days, and treated each one as an entity in itself. Each one runs a gamut of time, in which the design is one of flashbacks and flashforwards.

Another technique I have used in an effort to accurately depict life in America in the late nineteenth and early twentieth centuries is to include photographs taken during the time of the events described along with newspaper headlines, articles and advertisements of the era that have been preserved on microfiche. John Dos Passos conceived this technique some seventy years ago in his USA trilogy.

The last section in *The Black Hussars* is about police today and the politics that prevail throughout almost all law enforcement agencies. Political influence was shunned and, in fact, completely rejected by the early superintendents of the Pennsylvania State Police. They made every man on the Force adhere to this policy. In the modern world of political pull, political correctness and quotas, it is fascinating to come across the early rules governing the Pennsylvania State Police — any hint of political activity was enough to get a man dismissed from the force.

Neither pictures nor microfiche are used in this final part of the story for we know what the world looks like today and what prices are. Headlines and pictures as used in the earlier chapters would be superfluous.

Charles Boyle, 1999

THE BLACK HUSSARS

INTRODUCTION

Established in 1905, the Pennsylvania State Police was the nation's first state police force; a pioneering institution that set the standard for every highway patrol and state police department in the United States.

"History," wrote Voltaire, "is only a record of crimes and misfortunes." The history of the Pennsylvania State Police is indeed "... a record of crimes and misfortunes..." especially the misfortunes of the immigrants, coupled in those early days with the honor and courage of the men wearing the black uniforms.

The Force was ostensibly created to bring law to the rural areas of the Commonwealth at a time when there was staggering lawlessness and little or no police protection. The districts selected to quarter the four Troops of State Police, however, were not in the central or farming regions of the state. They just "happened" to be put in areas close to where hundreds of thousands of foreign immigrants lived in company towns and worked in coal mines. These miners often went on strikes that frequently led to violence. When the Coal and Iron Police were unable to handle the rioting strikers, the National Guard had to be called out. Calling out the Guard put a heavy burden on the state's taxpayers.

The newly formed State Police first began to patrol the regions to which they were assigned in early 1906 and word quickly spread about their toughness and ability to act forcefully and decisively. Immigrants from Eastern Europe began calling the troopers "Black Hussars," for, in their minds, the men on the black horses in the black uniforms reminded them of the soldiers who enforced the laws of their native countries. But once the "Hussars" came on the scene, the National Guard was never again mustered to maintain law and order during a labor strike. The troopers saved the state an enormous amount of money. A cynic might reasonably argue that economics, not citizen protection, was the real impetus for establishing the nation's first State Police Force — its raison d'être.

It's true that the troopers were used to stop riots and keep strikers under control in labor disputes, but their record in fighting crime also was outstanding. During the first few years of their existence, the "Black Hussars" arrested murderers, kidnappers, rapists, and scores of other kinds of criminals by the thousands.

Each of the four Troops was comprised of sixty men, some of whom were assigned to sub-stations in the Troop's region. This enabled a small force of men on horseback to provide a presence and protection to people in an area covering some 45,000 square miles of rural Pennsylvania. Whatever underlying motive was behind the decision to form a State Police Force — to fight labor violence or to fight crime — both purposes were served far beyond the expectations of the populace, the press, and the state government.

Before the Pennsylvania State Police Force was a dozen years old, newspaper articles, pamphlets and books — even a short movie in 1914 — were praising the "Black Hussars." The most notable and influential book written was Katherine Mayo's *Justice for All,* published in 1916. President Theodore Roosevelt liked the thrust of the book so much that he wrote its Forward.

Miss Mayo, who lived in rural upstate New York, which was also suffering from lawlessness, began to lobby for a State Police Force in her state. Roosevelt believed every state should copy Pennsylvania's plan to fight rural crime. Using her book, and armed with the research she put into it, Miss Mayo and Teddy Roosevelt went before the New York legislature and vigorously presented their case. The result was the creation of the New York State Police, the second such uniformed force in the United States. It happened just one year after the publication of Miss Mayo's book and twelve years after the "Black Hussars" came onto the stage of the nation.

Other states soon followed the Keystone and Empire states in forming their own State Police. In 1921, New Jersey called upon H. Norman Schwarzkopf, the father of Desert Storm hero General Norman Schwarzkopf, to be the first Superintendent of its new State Police Force. Schwarzkopf was a graduate of West Point and served with distinction in World War One. He also was only twenty-five years old at the time of his appointment, the youngest head of a State Police Force in the country.

As the Pennsylvania State Police went through its first decade basking in the esteem of the mainstream press, other publications were being distributed throughout the state telling a different story about the black-clad men on horseback. Much of this prose denounced what the writers called "The Pennsylvania Cossacks," or "the murderous Cossacks." The authors of these derogatory pieces were, for the most part, radical labor leaders or politicians. They opposed the legislation that created the Force, and then wanted the State Police disbanded from the moment they came into the world. Obviously the attacks failed and the Force continues to survive nearly a century after its birth.

If, as some say, that the economics of labor unrest was the underlying reason for establishing the Pennsylvania State Police, we can take heart in the outcome, not only for Pennsylvania, but also for the other states of the union that eventually followed the lead of the Keystone State. But to fully appreciate what the original troopers did and under what conditions, it is necessary to understand what American life and economic conditions were at the onset of the 20th century.

Newspapers printed in 1905 advertised good wool suits for men that cost ten dollars. A home could be purchased for under a thousand dollars. Obviously, a dollar doesn't go as far today as it did one hundred years ago. On the other hand, people didn't have as many dollars to spend one hundred years ago. Help Wanted ads offered "wonderful opportunities for girls for steady, easy work in nice clean factories" where they could earn as much as $4.50 to $8 a week (no doubt a six-day week in those days). Depending on whether they were paid $4.50 or $8 a week for their fifty hours of labor, they were either earning less or slightly more than the minimum wage paid to workers in 1999 - for one hour of work.

Through the first part of this century, a Pennsylvania State Trooper was paid $700 a year and a coal miner earned, on average, $400 a year. The trooper's pay amounted to about $20,000 a year in 1999 dollars and, at first glance, it would appear the trooper was still coming up short compared to what trooper's are paid today (about $35,000). But there is another big difference between the economics of the past and those of the present. Taxes in the early 1900's were practically non-existent. No income tax. No sales tax. Very few hidden taxes. A person who earned $700 a year in 1905 kept it all and, indeed, could buy a good wool suit for ten dollars. An unmarried coal miner lived "comfortably" on $200 a year and still had enough left over to either save or spend on entertainment, usually in a saloon.

The budget for the Pennsylvania State Police during its first decade of existence averaged $280,000 per year. That would hardly pay the salaries of the top officers in the Force today which has an annual budget of more than $150 million. State government had few agencies and a very low budget in 1905 and offered very few services. The counties provided a "poor house," a sheriff, a county jail, and a courthouse. The communities and the churches provided the schools. The governor who created the Pennsylvania State Police, Samuel Pennypacker, had a staff of two people, a male secretary and a woman stenographer. It would not be an easy task to count how many people serve a governor today.

An understanding and appreciation of the economics of that era helps to put into perspective the tremendous cost of a widespread coal miners strike. And not only the cost in dollars, but also the hardship rendered on both the miners with wives and children living on the edge of survival, as well as the consumers. For the first third of this century a large percentage of the population heated their homes and cooked their food with coal. A big coal strike had about the same deleterious effect then that cutting off electricity and gas would have on Americans today, and not just in Pennsylvania, but in the rest of the nation, for coal was the main source of energy in homes and in factories.

The purchasing power of the dollar has seen many changes over the course of the past century, but regardless of the current value of the dollar, the mark, the pound or yen, money still, as it has throughout history, makes the world go 'round. As someone once said, it wasn't the fair face of Helen that launched a thousand ships on Troy. It was economics. The

Greeks wanted control of the Dardanelles and the Trojans had to be disposed of. And it wasn't crime alone, but also the economics of labor unrest that gave birth to the Pennsylvania State Police.

THE BLACK HUSSARS

PART I

THE MAN ON THE HILL

THE BLACK HUSSARS

> "...come on along,
> come on along,
> hear Alexander's Ragtime band ...

... from the microfiche...

PRESIDENT STARTS TWO MONTHS' TRIP TO THE SOUTHWEST – AFTER BIG GAME IN THE MOUNTAINS

Washington – With cheers and good wishes resounding through Pennsylvania Station, President Theodore Roosevelt left today on a special train for a trip through the Southwest. The nation's Chief Executive will make notable addresses at several places en route to San Antonio where he will attend a Rough Riders reunion, and thence dive into the vastness of Texas, Oklahoma, and Colorado.

New York Times 1905

> *... come on along,*
> *come on along,*
> *it's the best band in the land."*

" *... New Jersey town jails young lady for 50 days for doing the turkey trot ... 15 girls fired in Philadelphia when their employer found them turkey-trotting on their lunch break... "*

3

FATAL SHOOTING AMONG IMMIGRANTS

A Slavic christening at Jamison Mine No. 2, four miles from Latrobe, ended in the usual tragedy yesterday morning, one man being killed and four seriously wounded. The festivities started Saturday evening at the home of John Boreko, where a keg of beer had been provided for each guest, in addition to jugs of whiskey. A fight started and revolvers were brought into play. This is the fifth time in the past four months that people have either been killed, wounded or both at Slavish celebrations.

Johnstown Tribune 1905

1.

Although he was relaxed, his head was held high and his back was ramrod straight. The solitary Trooper sat in the saddle gazing down into the sunny valley from the top of a hill in Schuylkill County, just on the outskirts of a small mining community. Like the color of his horse, the man's uniform was completely black. In spite of the warm weather, he had on black boots, whipcord riding britches, a military tunic reaching from his hips up to just below his chin. A black Sam Brown belt was around his waste and he had a black holster with a .38 revolver attached to the belt. Black horsehide gloves — they were called gauntlets — reached halfway to his elbows. His head was covered with a black reinforced helmet with leather chinstraps similar to the kind worn by London Bobbies except for the large silver emblem on the front of the helmet. A hickory baton, more than two feet long, hung from the saddle and was secured by two-inch wide leather straps. The top of the "riot stick" was just inches from his hands that were resting on the saddle horn.

In the valley below, about five hundred people, men women and children, were holding a picnic on this warm June Sunday in 1916. A large portion of the crowd was made up of young bachelors who worked in the anthracite mines in eastern Pennsylvania. The other men, also coal miners, were at the picnic with their wives and children, enjoying a day off from their backbreaking labor. Sunday was the one day of rest for the miners who spent the other six days of the week below the surface, laboring ten to twelve hours a day, week after week, month after month. A year's work would pay them, on average, about $400. Almost every penny the married men earned was earmarked at inflated prices toward rent for the company-owned houses they lived in, and for food they had to buy at the company-owned store.

It was not an easy life, but it was better than what they had left behind in Eastern Europe, and there was hope for the future, if not for them, at least for their children. America, after all, was "the land of the free," ruled by law and not by the whim of a Czar whose mercurial demands were enforced by sword wielding Cossacks. These immigrants and their American-born children were mostly from peasant stock and unskilled urban poor. For centuries they had endured the hardships of enemy invasions, ruthless occupations, enslavement, overtaxing and early death at the hands of the invaders and their own governments.

The horseman looked down on the scene, a melee of screeching children, running after hoops and each other. The parents were sitting serenely amid the babble, eating sausages and potatoes and drinking beer. Most of the men had taken off their coats and collars, and even rolled up their sleeves. All too soon the warm summer would end and the fogs of autumn would descend, heralding the long winter. It was small wonder that these working people deserted their cramped and dingy homes to spend a day like this in a country meadow.

The man on the horse was about to turn away and ride off from the pleasant panorama below, when suddenly a fight broke out where only moments ago it was a peaceful outing. Sides were quickly taken and, in less than 30 seconds, knives were drawn, clubs were snatched up from the fallen branches of trees, and a battle erupted involving most of the men and even some of the women. A shrieking brawl was on the verge of turning into a bloody riot.

The horseman sat for a second, as still as a statue. Then, drawing his baton, he nudged his small black steed down the hill, heading toward the battle at a slow trot when someone in the crowd spotted him. Shouts rang out piercing the din of the battle, "Hussars! Hussars!"

The words were like magic. The fighting instantly stopped as the rioters dropped their clubs, sliding away from where they were dumped, while more than a dozen other men ran off into the woods.

The "Hussar" brought his horse to a walk and, without saying a word or turning his head, he casually wended his way through the crowd, stopping only once. He leaned down from the saddle and looked into the face of a tow-headed twelve year-old boy. The youth was almost shaking as he stared back into the clear, blue eyes of the severely clad young man on the black horse.

"What's your name?" the "Hussar" asked in a friendly tone.

"Alex," the boy mumbled in reply, his eyes wide in fear.

The man in black smiled slightly, turned his horse, and rode back through the subdued crowd, up the hill and out of sight.

The "Hussar" who singly rode into a mob of armed and fighting men, dispersing them without a word, was one of a small group of superbly trained and dedicated men assigned to four strategically located Troops in eastern and western Pennsylvania. They were called various names by immigrants and by the press. But to many immigrants in the early part of the century, especially those from Eastern Europe, they were the "Black Hussars," or "Cossacks." These horsemen dressed in black reminded the immigrants of the King's soldiers or the Czar's Cossacks back in their native lands: soldiers who too often rode them down with slashing swords. The horseman who rode into the picnic area, however, was not part of a military force to suppress the people, but rather to help them, if they needed assistance, and to impartially enforce the laws of the State. He was a member of the Pennsylvania State Police Force.

While this took place in the valley, Professor Bertram Simonds was standing on another nearby hill watching the entire episode unfold.

"I tell you," Simonds later recounted, *"you won't find one reputable man, woman, or child in this county who will say a derogatory word of the Force.... they will defend the home of the poorest in this county as quickly and with just as much vigor as they will the homes of the rich ... they will act more promptly, use less violence, and bring a man into arrest more easily than any other force known. They won't club someone because he is drunk. A man is to be tried in this term of court who they followed thirty-five hundred miles. And they got him! And it did not cost the county a cent!"*

Simonds' lavish praise of the Black Hussars was not uncommon in 1916, although there were others who were just as resolutely against them. Pro or con, however, emotions about the force were not tepid.

The Act creating the Pennsylvania State Police in 1905 was now eleven years old. The Troopers had been patrolling the State for ten years.

But the seeds that eventually grew into this elite Force were planted forty years earlier in 1865 when another legislative Act was passed creating an entirely different kind of "lawman" ... the infamous Coal and Iron Police.

.... from the microfiche ...

SHERMAN MARCHES THROUGH THE CAROLINAS

Dispatch, March 1865 - General William T. Sherman has completed his "March to the Sea." His 100,000-man army, living off the land, has triumphantly made its way to the coast, cutting a wide swath of destruction through the South and piercing "the shell of the C.S.A. and it's all hollow inside."

LEE SURRENDERS TO GRANT

"Oh, I'm a good old rebel!
Now that's just what I am;
For this "Fair Land of Freedom
I do not care a damn.
I'm glad I fit against it,
I only wisht we'd won,
And I don't want no pardon
For nothin that I've done."

WAR COMING TO END - RECONSTRUCTION TO BEGIN

LINCOLN ASSASSINATED AT FORD'S THEATER

Washington DC- April 14, 1865 – The young man leaped from the theater box onto the stage, glared at the audience, and shouted, *"Sic semper tyrannis!"* Ever thus to tyrants! The crowd in Ford's theater was puzzled until a woman's scream rang out: *"He has shot the President!"*

> *"I can't take up my musket*
> *And fight 'em now no more;*
> *But I ain't gonna love 'em,*
> *And that is certain sure;*
> *And I don't want no pardon*
> *For what I was and am;*
> *And I won't be reconstructed,*
> *And I don't care a damn."*

The assassination of Lincoln by the well-known actor John Wilkes Booth, at the moment of victory for the Union forces, aroused a display of mass emotion. A special funeral train bore the dead President's body home to Springfield, Illinois across a mourning country **"through day and night,"** said Whitman, **"with the great cloud darkening the land."**

> *"When Johnny comes marching home again,*
> *Hoorah! Hoorah!*
> *We'll give him a hearty welcome then,*
> *Hoorah! Hoorah!"*

9

2.

Except for the horrors of the Civil War, nothing so affected the tranquillity of the United States in the second half of the nineteenth century as did the Industrial Revolution. The nation changed from an agrarian society to an industry and business economy. By 1865 the factory system was fully established and, says the *Pennsylvania Manual, "the foundations of the State's industrial greatness were well laid."* As well as wealth for some, the change brought destruction, disorder and death that shook much of society for decades.

Farming in Pennsylvania did not fully disappear with the advent of the industrial revolution. To this day, some of the most beautiful farms in the world continue to thrive in the southeastern part of the state in Lancaster County. This is Amish country, where the "plain people" continue their way of life much as they did in the 19th century. The central part of the state, above Harrisburg, as well as other sections, also remained primarily agrarian. But there was no stopping the inexorable advance of machinery and the fuel to run it. The location of the state and its rich resources would make Pennsylvania the leader in manufacturing well into the 20th century. Along with New England, it assumed leadership in the textile industry with more than two hundred textile mills. Other important fields of enterprise included leather making, lumbering, shipbuilding and paper manufacturing. But mostly steel, iron and "king coal" made many a millionaire and sent thousands of men to an early grave.

At the time of the Civil War, the State rolled half of the nation's iron, which gave impetus to the development of the railroad age by furnishing the rails and locomotives. The iron and steel industries of the Keystone State provided the industrial strength that enabled the North to preserve the Union. By the end of the war, the Cambria Works at Johnstown was the largest steel mill in the country, eventually stretching for ten miles along the Stoney Creek and Conemaugh Rivers. The mills were fed by nearby coal mines in Cambria, Somerset and Indiana counties and, in turn, both mills and mines fed their waste into the two rivers and other streams as well. The major steel and iron cities of the State were Pittsburgh and Johnstown in the west and Bethlehem in the east.* In these cities, thousands of smokestacks spewed a cloak of darkness into the skies and a layer of soot on everything below.

Shortly after the turn of the 20th century, a labor leader wrote in a pamphlet: "Pennsylvania unquestionably leads all other states in her industrial development. ...this state but a century ago, enveloped in her beautiful mantle of green, her thousands of miles of timber, her sparkling, well-stocked rivers of fish... was indeed a fertile field for the serpent-like monster of capitalism...it has denuded the forests, poisoned the streams...turned thousands of square miles of the green, velvet-like pasture into barren black desert."

Applying that description to the entire state was grand hyperbole. Most of the state retained its beauty, but there were pockets of denuded nature, gritty dirt, and shabby dwellings. The steel cities had their mansions and middle-class sections, but they were mostly dreary, dingy towns with a plenitude of saloons to slake the thirst of the steelworkers and a church on almost every corner to provide solace for their wives.

As bad as it was for the men in the steel mills, it was even worse for the coal miners in the last half of the 19th century. They lived in company towns called "patches," clusters of company-owned houses along a dirt street huddled under the shadow of a giant colliery. These two-room, unpainted houses had one-inch thick clapboard walls and dirt floors. Each room had one narrow window covered with cardboard in a futile effort to keep out the wind, rain, and snow. They were opened only in warm weather. As many as twelve people lived in these shacks. Heating and cooking came from a small stove. The fuel for the stove was coal gathered up by the wives and daughters of the miners from slag heaps or from alongside the railroad tracks; the spillage from the loaded coal cars as they passed the houses on their way to the main line of the railroad.

---

*Bethlehem Steel was founded in Bethlehem, PA in 1905 by merging nine companies that made gun forgings and ships. These nine ironworks formed the base for what was to become the second largest steel company in America.

WOMEN KEEP THE HOME FIRES BURNING
circa 1900

(1) Women and children gathered coal from the gigantic slag heaps that dotted the coal mining areas.

(2) They also picked up coal from alongside the railroad tracks and took it home for cooking and heating.

(3) Wash Day, usually a Monday, the women gathered around a water hydrant that served the water needs of the community.

(4) Dressed in their finest clothes, the immigrant miners and their families gathered on Sunday afternoons to talk and enjoy each other's company in this strange land.

All- (Courtesy Applied Arts Publishing)

The sons in these families would go to work in the mines when they were as young as seven years old. In Schuylkill County alone there were 22,000 miners in the 1870s; 5,500 of them were boys between seven and sixteen. As long as the husband or sons were able to work in the mines, the family could stay in the company-owned house. If they were killed or seriously injured, which happened frequently, the family was thrown out to face the elements or accept the charity of relatives.

The towns, or patches, were completely the property of the mine owners and this included the company store where the miners were compelled to buy their food. The miners called the stores "pluck me." The prices were at least twenty percent higher than at stores in nearby towns and the miner bought his food on the "book." The Philadelphia *North American* wrote: *"...if a miner with a family of eight or ten... once gets into debt with the 'pluck me,' he remains in debt until his sons have grown up, and then their earnings, perhaps, will help to decrease the burden ...there are families who for ten years have never received a dollar in cash for their labor."*

When times were hard, which was often, a miner's pay dropped to fifty cents a day, and there were desperate men with hungry families who gladly worked fourteen hours to get that. Those fourteen-hour days were not only backbreaking, but, deadly. In one year, in one county, 112 miners were killed and 339 permanently injured from fires and cave-ins. The mines were poorly ventilated, reeking with standing gas, decaying timber, and stagnant water. As for the pay, at the best of times it was seven dollars for a sixty-hour week in the mid-nineteenth century.

Talking about wages for the miners in terms of dollars, however, is presumptive. Most of the time the miner received a "bobtail" check at the end of the month which was good for absolutely nothing. It merely showed his current debt at the company store.

The miner crawled underground in mud and water breathing coal dust and powder smoke. He emerged from the living hell below - if not blasted to death or mutilated - only to find his rest in a hovel barely fit for habitation. Meantime, the mine owners and investors were reaping enor-

13

mous profits and living in mansions.

The only weapon the miner had was to withhold his labor, cutting into the profits of the owners and hitting them in the pocket book. The mine owners tried to overcome that problem by manipulating immigration laws that flooded the coal regions with foreigners willing to work at any wage. In the 1860s, these immigrants were mainly Irish who swarmed to the United States to escape the lingering aftermath of the Great Potato Famine of the 1840s. Thousands of them settled into the hard coal regions of Eastern Pennsylvania and were soon victims of exploitation by the coal barons.

... from the microfiche ...

London News ... English landlords in Ireland find it cheaper to ship off tenants to America than pay their taxes as the potato famine drags on. Thousands set sail on "Coffin Ships." One in five die en-route and are thrown overboard.

> *"The weeping mother abandoned ship,*
> *to where her child had gone.*
> *The dry-eyed Captain smoked his pipe,*
> *and the sailing ship sailed on."*

Like the English and Welsh miners they were replacing, the Irish also tried to form unions in a push for better pay and working conditions. Their efforts failed completely and many of them turned to the violence of the Molly Maguires. This was a secret organization that was formed originally in Ireland in 1843 and named for a widow who was killed because she was unable to pay her debts. The purpose of the "Mollies" was to frighten rent collectors, landlords, and others who oppressed the poverty-stricken population of the Emerald Isle. Irish immigrants brought the organization to the United States. In retaliation against the mine owners for what they considered to be unbearable working conditions and pay, members of the Molly Maguires attacked the mine bosses and committed acts of sabotage on the mines.

The local county sheriffs and town constables were unable to protect the property of the mining companies, so the corporations put pressure on the politicians. In 1865, the Pennsylvania General Assembly passed an Act that created the Railroad Police. This was followed, in the spring of 1866, with passage of another Act authorizing " ... *all corporations, firms, or individuals owning, leasing, or being in possession of any colliery, furnace, or rolling mill, within this Commonwealth ...* " to appoint, pay and maintain their own police forces by simply applying to the State for commissions. For one dollar per man, the commission gave these men police power.

Thus was born the Coal and Iron Police, many of whom were no more than gunmen, thugs, and adventurers. These "lawmen" were not responsible for their actions to the public, but rather to the railroad, steel, and coal barons who hired them. In theory, the powers of this new law enforcement agency were limited to protecting the property of the mines, steel plants, and railroads. In actual practice, there was no limit to the powers they usurped. After all, the hovels the miners lived in were the property of their bosses and the Coal and Iron Police had no qualms over intruding on the occupants. This new "police force" carried riot sticks, revolvers and Winchester rifles, and they never hesitated to use them.

THE COAL AND IRON POLICE

Badge No. 4 of the
P&R Coal...

On September 10, 1897, the Luzerne County sheriff and 87 deputies attacked striking miners at the Lattimer Patch, a small mining community in Eastern Pennsylvania. Eighteen miners were killed and thirty-six people were wounded. It became known as the "Lattimer Massacre". There was a similar massacre at Sugarloaf, a small coal mining patch near Hazleton. As the 20th Century came on the scene, conditions got worse. In January of 1900, the Philadelphia & Reading Coal and Iron Police train was rushed to the North Franklin Colliery at Treverton where labor trouble developed. The P & R Coal and Iron Police was the only law enforcement agency in the world that had its own private police train. The train was composed of two coaches, a commissary and a sleeping car. The cadre consisted of 25 "police officers" and a Lieutenant.

(Courtesy Applied Arts Publishing)

Whenever there was labor unrest, the "State stepped in to show *its impartial justice,"* Katherine Mayo wrote, *"by selling its authority to the special interests of the corporations."* Instead of bringing law and order to the coal fields and steel centers, the strikes and vandalism grew more violent.

"In the prison cell I sit thinking, mother dear, of you,
And our happy home so far, far away.
And the tears they fill my eyes, 'spite of all that I can do,
Tho' I try to cheer my comrades and be gay."

THE BLACK HUSSARS

It was early in the morning on the first day of summer, June 21, 1877. The town of Pottsville, Pennsylvania was crowded with people who came to see the death of the Molly Maguires. Two young Irishmen dressed in their finest clothes, walked slowly down a brick path inside a walled courtyard. They spoke softly to each other as they pressed a red rose to their faces, inhaling deeply. They mounted the gallows in the yard, kissed the hands of a priest, blessed their friends, granted forgiveness to their enemies, and then were hanged.

Within two hours, four more Irishmen walked the same path and were also hanged. The sheriff originally planned to hang them all at the same time, but decided it would make a sight too grizzly to be tolerated.

In Mauch Chunk, forty miles to the east on this warm, pleasant summer day, four more Irishmen were hanged one-by-one in the corridor of Carbon County's new jail. Before the executions ended, twenty members of the Molly Maguires were hanged by the neck. It took as long as eight minutes for some of them to die from strangulation as improperly tied knots slipped on their necks.

With the exception of the execution of thirty-eight Sioux Indians at Mankato, Minnesota in 1862, the mass hanging of the "Mollies" was the largest ever held in the United States, exceeding the witch orgy of New England in pre-Revolutionary days.

For the Irish, this was "Black Thursday," when the first ten of the twenty convicted and condemned members of the Molly Maguires were executed, ending a reign of terror that swept the eastern Pennsylvania coal fields for more than a decade. Fewer than six hundred men, banded together under the aegis of the secret society with its roots in Ireland, grew so powerful that they could commit any crime, secure in the knowledge that alibis would be furnished them, that few witnesses had the courage to testify against them, and that no juror would convict them for fear of being murdered. What began as a militant labor organization ended as a terrorist society involved in criminal activities.

Scarcely had a decade gone by since the formation of the infamous Coal and Iron Police when the equally infamous Molly Maguires were smashed. Between the years 1862 and 1875, there were, in Schuylkill County alone, 142 unsolved murders and 212 felonious assaults. Many of the victims were mine superintendents and foremen who incurred the wrath of a "Molly" or the friend of a "Molly." It wasn't hard for anyone in a supervisory position at the mines to find himself a target of the Molly Maguires. The mine owners crushed the unions and the Mollies crushed the agents of the mine owners — until the Coal and Iron Police, with the help of a Pinkerton Detective, put the Molly Maguires out of business.

Arthur Conan Doyle used the Molly Maguires as the basis for his work *The Valley of Fear* with Sherlock Holmes.

THE COAL INDUSTRY ABOVE GROUND
These are collieries and breakers at the turn of the century

This one with the horse and buggy is the No. 9 breaker of the Lehigh Coal Company in Panther Valley. It was built in 1876 and abandoned in 1910. Many Molly Maquires worked at this breaker.

This breaker with the trains in the foreground is Sugar Notch Colliery near Wilkes-Barre, PA in 1910

(Courtesy Applied Arts Publishing)

19

... from the microfiche ...

FEDERAL TROOPS USED
TO PUT DOWN RAILROAD STRIKES

Pittsburgh — 1877 – "Railroad strikes have broken out in several cities. Riot-bound soldiers of the Sixth Maryland Regiment battled through Baltimore toward the railroad station, firing point-blank at strikers and un-employed sympathizers. Citywide rioting lasting four days has taken 50 lives.

Meanwhile, here in Pennsylvania, mushrooming flames billowed up in the Pittsburgh freight yards. A wall of fire three miles long destroyed installations valued at millions of dollars. Sixteen persons have been killed by militia gunfire. Eight soldiers and the Allegheny County sheriff have been killed by rioters. 650 National Guardsmen have been routed by a mob and the fire. For the first time since Jackson's day, federal troops have been called up to quell strikes."

SPECIAL ELECTORAL COMMISSION
DECLARES HAYES PRESIDENT

ARMY AUTHORIZED TO PURSUE MEXICAN BANDITS
ACROSS MEXICAN BORDER

Queen Victoria proclaimed empress of India

Socialist Labor party formed in the United States

"When a man is steady and sober, and ...finds himself in debt for a common living, something must be wrong." Thus does one worker express the confusion and the hardship besetting workers everywhere.

Radical Johann Most offers one cure for all employers:
"Extirpate the miserable brood."

New York, 1877 - There is a grim truth in a chilling remark by tycoon Jay Gould: *"I can hire one half of the working class to kill the other half."*

Mine fire in Avondale, Pennsylvania.
Whole shift perishes leaving 59 widows and 10 orphans.

HARD TIMES FOR MINERS —
YEAR-LONG STRIKE IN VAIN

"Anthracite miners go on strike as the mine operators cut wages. Operators respond to the strike by importing workers from Europe and by using the Coal and Iron Police to protect them. The strikebreaking tactics set off a small, vicious and violent war. Labor loses as the miners are starved into submission".

... from the microfiche...

"Buffalo Bill" Cody forms first Wild West show

Mark Twain's "Huckleberry Finn" published

Waterman perfects the fountain pen.

REPUBLICAN NOMINATION OF BLAINE CAUSES "MUG-WUMP" BOLT TO CLEVELAND

Washington, 1884 - GOP chides Grover Cleveland for his affair with Maria Halpin by pushing baby carriages through the streets chanting;

"Ma! Ma! Where's my Pa?"

CLEVELAND ELECTED PRESIDENT

Democrats answer GOP: *"Gone to the White House, Ha! Ha! Ha!"*

... from the microfiche ...

Cocaine developed as surgical anesthetic

Indian warfare ends with capture of Geronimo

BEN HARRISON ELECTED PRESIDENT
BY NARROW MARGIN

Washington, 1888 – Grover Cleveland outpolls Benjamin Harrison in popular vote but electoral system gives Presidency back to GOP.

DAM BREAKS ABOVE JOHNSTOWN!!

WALL OF WATER WIPES OUT CITY —
MORE THAN TWO THOUSAND DIE IN FLOOD

Johnstown, PA 1889 – "The earthen dam at the South Fork reservoir, 12 miles upstream from this steel city, gave out as heavy rains weakened the structure and a forty-foot high wall of water roared down the valley toward Johnstown. Within minutes more than two thousand people were killed and the city practically destroyed. The dam was incorporated under the name of the South Fork Country Club, a private fishing resort owned by Pittsburgh's steel company owners, managers and bankers."

"By the sea, by the sea, by the beautiful sea,
You and me, you and me,
Oh! how happy we'll be..."

Cornelius Vanderbilt has converted four million dollars into a 70-room "cottage," the terminology used to describe summer homes by the elite. Set on an 11-acre promontory at Newport, Rhode Island, the mansion is named The Breakers. One observer describes its over-all effect as "paralyzing." Two of its largest rooms were designed and built in France, torn apart, shipped to Newport and carefully rebuilt by the French workmen brought over for that purpose. Another Vanderbilt, William, has built Marble House, close to The Breakers and comparably opulent. William's daughter Consuelo is to be married to a titled Englishman. The Vanderbilts got a Duke; the Duke got $2.5 million.

CLEVELAND ELECTED PRESIDENT - AGAIN

Washington, 1892 – "Winning by 400,000 popular votes, Grover Cleveland is the nation's President once again."

23

4.

WILSON PRICE

It is a close-knit group, this little band of brothers who know each other so well.   "We all depend on each other and go to the limit knowing another Trooper is there to back us all the way."

Lt. Wilson Price one day said with almost tearful sympathy to a village constable who had just committed an act of uncommon dullness:

"Why, you dear soul, if all your brains were nitroglycerin there wouldn't be enough inside your head to blow off your hat."

The Lieutenant's Sergeant, who overheard this comment, managed to keep from laughing in the presence of the constable but, when he was transferred to the other side of the state, he told the story to his new Captain without mentioning any names.

"Did Price say that?" The officer asked. When the sergeant nodded yes, the Captain grinned and said, "I thought so. Price does say things like that. I served with him in China."

The Black Hussars never talked about their Army service, but the records in the War Department note that Price was awarded the Certificate of Merit "for most distinguished gallantry in action against the Chinese at the City of Tien Tsin, July 13, 1900."   The citation was supposed to have been the Medal of Honor.

Wilson C. Price came into the world in County Antrim, Ireland, in 1881, one of nine children born to Alexander and Ellen Price. When he was four years old, the family set sail for America seeking, as so many other Irish families, a better life in the New World. Price celebrated his fifth birthday during the voyage.

As the ship sailed up the Delaware River and neared Philadelphia, a severe storm pounded it and the vessel began to flounder. Another ship rescued the passengers as they abandoned the sinking craft. The Price family lost all its possessions and was set ashore at Philadelphia on August 18, 1886.

When he reached his teens, young Wilson Price became an apprentice machinist in an effort to help out his family, but he was determined to get an education as well. Price enrolled in the International Correspondence School at Scranton and continued to take academic courses by mail throughout his working years in the machine shop. This all came to an end in 1899. The United States, in the wake of the Spanish-American War, was sucked into another war against insurgents in the Philippines. Price, seeking adventure, joined the Army a couple of months shy of his 18th birthday and then was shipped to the Pacific.

As an infantryman, Price saw action in the Philippines and then in China during the Boxer Rebellion where he was recommended for the Congressional Medal of Honor for outstanding courage and actions above and beyond the call of duty.

More than two decades later, when Price became the first Commander of the Highway Patrol, a newly formed arm of the State Police, a Pennsylvania Congressman looked into Price's military record and came up with the details of Price's adventures in the Philippines and China.

Price *"... joined his company at San Fernando, Luzon, in September of 1899 and took part in the advance on and capture of Angeles. There were eleven engagements with the enemy in that advance and the fighting to capture Tarlac, then the capital of the Philippine Republic and the headquarters of the resurgent forces. Price fought in the Philippines for nine months."*

In June of 1900, a bloody uprising broke out in northern China as a movement got underway against the spread of Western and Japanese influence. The movement was started by a secret Chinese society called *I-ho-chu'uan,* (Righteous and Harmonious Fists). Westerners nicknamed the society members *Boxers*. The Boxers were determined to destroy everything foreign in China. They slaughtered Chinese Christians, missionaries and other persons from foreign countries. When foreign diplomats in Peking sent out a call for troops, the Manchu government declared war against the foreign powers.

On June 21st, Boxers and Chinese government troops besieged the

25

legations, the official residences of the foreign diplomats in Peking. This action by the Chinese prompted a military move by the foreign powers. Army and marine forces from eight nations were sent to China in an effort to rescue the trapped European, American and Japanese citizens in the large compound.

The 9th Infantry (Price's outfit) was ordered to China from the Philippines to protect American citizens and to relieve the U.S. Legation. On July 9, 1900, the transport Logan, bearing the 9th Infantry and other troops, arrived at Taku, China; the troops were disembarked and proceeded to Tien Tsen where it was found that a state of war existed between the Western/Japanese powers and the Boxers and the Imperial Chinese Government.

"On the morning of July 13," according to Price's military record, *"the allied forces, of which the 9th Infantry was a part, attacked the walled city of Tien Tsen. During the battle that ensued, the 9th was ordered to the right flank of the Japanese in an effort to quell a heavy enfilading fire. This movement was hampered and eventually stopped by a series of water-filled ditches and, as ammunition ran low, the Regiment found itself in a very dangerous position. At this point, Lt. Lewis B. Dawson, adjutant of the 1st Battalion, who had been sent to the rear by his Commanding Officer in an effort to secure reinforcements and ammunition, came running across the field to the front line. He was seen to stagger and fall, then regain his feet and come forward; again he seemed to receive a heavy blow and fell, was unable to rise but began to crawl forward and fell into a ditch near where Price was lying and firing toward the Chinese line. Price immediately went to the assistance of Lt. Lawton and found that he had been severely wounded in the right arm, the right breast, the foot and the head. While Price was administering first aid to the officer, the Chinese began an encircling movement that gave them direct fire down the ditch in which the Americans had sought shelter. When Price noted this he immediately began, with the tools at hand, a mess pan and bayonet, to dig a trench and traverse for the protection of Lt. Lawton. As the work on this trench progressed, Price was able to bring two other wounded men into its protection; one of these*

men, *Private Hammons of Company F, had a gunshot wound of the groin and the other, Private Packett from Company C, had a gunshot wound of the jaw.*

"Through the medium of this crudely constructed trench and traverse, Price was able to protect these men from the Chinese fire and undoubtedly saved their lives. When eventually relieved of their position, the wounded men were evacuated to the hospital and Lt. Lawton recommended the Medal of Honor for Price's heroic efforts on July 13, 1900. Lawton cited as witnesses Major J. M. Lee, 9th Infantry and Private Packett, Company C, 9th Infantry, and himself. For some unaccountable reason the recommendation was changed by Lt. Col. C.A. Coolidge to read 'Certificate of Merit' instead of Medal of Honor. Price went on to fight in the battles of Yang-Tsun, Ho-Sie-Wu, Matow, Tung-Chow and Peking."

On August 14th, 1900, fifty-five days after the siege began, the allied forces crushed the uprising and a settlement called *The Boxer Protocol* was signed.

After returning home, Price was presented the United States Certificate of Merit by President Theodore Roosevelt on March 10, 1902.

Leading a charge against some Wobblies a few years later must have seemed rather tame to the gallant Price who eventually rose to be Superintendent of the Pennsylvania State Police. Price died in 1937.

5.

Urging their horses at full speed, sixteen Black Hussars in double file, led by Lieutenant Wilson C. Price, rode over fields and culm banks, jumping ditches and fences in an effort to end a reign of terror inflicted by one union upon another union. The troopers were racing toward a meeting hall in the town of Old Forge, a coal mining community near Wilkes-Barre in eastern Pennsylvania. More than 250 tough, radical men were in the hall. A county sheriff and a few deputies were standing helplessly outside the meeting place. They were waiting for the Black Hussars and for what they hoped would be the end of the terror.

In the late summer of 1916, members of the United Mine Workers Union at Old Forge, Peckville and Dupont had been under siege for nearly a year by The International Workers of the World. The I.W.W., known as the "Wobblies," wanted the UMW members to quit their union and join the Wobblies. Under severe pressure, some of them did. The sheriff of the county believed he could contain the frequent outbursts of trouble, but it continued to escalate. UMW members, who refused to leave their own organization and join the hated "Reds," were being attacked on their way to work. Even their young sons, breaker boys in the mines, were threatened, beaten, and even shot at by the Wobblies. The greatest fear of the union men, however, was the dynamiting of their homes while they slept; one of the tactics used by the I.W.W.

In early September, the Wobblies continued to strike in Old Forge. They made no demands on the mine owners for higher wages or shorter hours but, with hundreds of their pickets thronging the streets of the town, they prevented the members of the United Mineworkers Union from going to their jobs. Men were being beaten and murder threats were frequent.

On September 11th, the I.W.W. held a meeting at which a resolution was passed decreeing that the sheriff and the leader of the State Police should be killed. This was too much for Sheriff Joseph Phillips. He knew perfectly well that the bloody resolution was no idle bravado, but would go into effect whenever the would-be assassins were offered a safe opportunity to carry out their plan. Phillips also learned the I.W.W. leaders planned to hold a meeting on September 14th intending to precipitate a general outbreak of strikes on the following day including the touching off of a "grand explosion" in a distant part of the county.

On the morning of the 14th, Lieutenant Price and the sixteen troopers in his detail were patrolling the streets of Old Forge, escorting UMW workers to their jobs. When this task was completed, Price led his men straight down the main street and out of the town toward the Wyoming County Barracks of the State Police. Once out of sight, however, he changed course and swung into the cover of a wooded area and made a detour of the town reaching a point a little over a mile away from the back of the hall where the I.W.W. was going to meet.

At eleven o'clock that morning, the Wobblies began to enter the hall. Mrs. Herman Schwartz, wife of the hall's owner, tried to stop them on the grounds that the sheriff had prohibited the meeting. The leader of the "Reds" shoved her aside saying, "The hell with the sheriff. We're going to meet here and no sheriff can stop us."

The Wobblies crowded into the hall, confident that no authority would interfere with their meeting.

Sheriff Phillips and two of his deputies were standing a short distance away from the hall watching the men file into the building. When it became evident that the meeting was underway, Phillips sent one of his deputies to fetch Lieutenant Price. As soon as he got the word, Price and his men leapt into their saddles and charged into the town. Two troopers, ducking low and with their riot batons drawn, rode their horses straight into the meeting hall. Five others, also with riot sticks drawn, circled the rear door. Three more troopers, urging their horses, forced the mob on the streets back from the hall and held them a block away. The remaining six troopers, with Price at their head, sat their horses, batons in hand, at the front of the building.

As soon as the two troopers rode their horses into the hall, shouts rang out from the Wobblies. *"The Cossacks are here!"* *"Cossacks!"* Bedlam broke out and there was a wild scramble for the rear door. When they opened it, they came face to face with the State Police blocking the door with their horses. Surprised and shocked, there was a moment of complete silence. Then one of the leaders screamed, *"Let's get the troopers!"* and there was a rush toward the front door where the two Black Hussars who first entered the building sat firmly in their saddles and swung their batons at the approaching mob. Three more troopers rode their horses into the hall and the crowd began to drop their weapons onto the floor and huddle together.

While they were securely cribbed in the hall, the sheriff commandeered trucks, coal wagons and jitneys. The prisoners were then marched in a single file out to the waiting vehicles for the journey to jail. As they marched out, six troopers searched them, confiscating knives, stilettos and straight razors. An inspection of the hall after it was emptied of the mob turned up a large assortment of knives and daggers hastily dropped onto the rest of the litter where several hundred yellow I.W.W. buttons covered the floor like dandelions in a field. Not a single Wobblie button was found on any of the prisoners when they reached the jail.

As the makeshift caravan of paddy wagons moved through the streets, hundreds of United Mine Workers lined the sidewalks screaming epithets at the I.W.W. agitators. *"Kill them!"* *"Send them out of the country!"* *"Hanging's too good for them!"* The UMW union members were venting the fear, frustration and tension of the past year on the people who threatened to destroy their union. But the Wobblies had no reason to be afraid of the crowd lining the streets. A Black Hussar guarded each wagonload of them.

Two hundred and sixty-one prisoners sat in the motley vehicles. After a year of bloodshed and the expressed purpose to shed even more blood if they didn't get their way, the two hundred and sixty one Wobblies surrendered to Lt. Price and his sixteen young men of the Pennsylvania State Police.

"I can't say too much for the troopers," Sheriff Phillips said that

night. *"The way they worked today was something marvelous, and it shows the kind of men that are in that organization."*

The Wilkes-Barre correspondent for the Philadelphia *North American* wrote: *"The Cossacks' have been the men of the hour in Luzerne and Lackawanna counties, and their ability to meet all situations and fight when a fight is necessary has perhaps killed the I.W.W. activities in this region."*

... from the microfiche ...

PHILADELPHIA AND READING RAILROAD GOES BANKRUPT

500 BANKS CLOSE THEIR DOORS

16,000 BUSINESS HOUSES CLOSE DOWN

FULL SCALE ECONOMIC CRISIS WRACKS THE COUNTRY

CLEVELAND PICKS WRONG TIME TO WIN A SECOND TERM
More than 1,300 strikes paralyze the nation as the Gay Nineties get underway with a whimper.

... "nation degenerating into European conditions... tramps and millionaires..."

CENTURY WINDING DOWN WITH A BANG!

Chicago Haymarket Bombing by Anarchists – Twelve Killed, Many More Injured

---

THE BLACK HUSSARS

PRINCE OF PEACE

Andrew Carnegie
Was born in Dunfernline, Scotland
               came over to the States in an immigrant ship
worked as a bobbinboy in a textile factory
fired boilers
clerked in a bobbin factory at $2.50 a week
ran 'round Pittsburgh with telegrams as a Western Union messenger
learned the Morse code
was telegraph operator on the Pennsy lines
was a military telegraph operator in the Civil War and
always saved his pay;
whenever he had a dollar he invested it.
Andrew Carnegie started out buying Adams Express and Pullman stock
when they were in a slump;
he had confidence in railroads,
       he had confidence in communications,
             he had confidence in transportation,
Andrew Carnegie believed in iron,
       built bridges Bessemer plants blast furnaces rolling mills;
Andrew Carnegie believed in oil;
Andrew Carnegie believed in steel;
always saved his money
whenever he had a million dollars he invested it.
Andrew Carnegie became the richest man in the world
                     and died.
Bessemer Duquesne Rankin Pittsburgh Bethlehem Gary
Andrew Carnegie gave millions for peace
and libraries and scientific institutes and endowments
and thrift
whenever he made a billion dollars he endowed an institution
to promote universal peace
     always
     except in time of war.

                        Dos Passos, <u>42nd Parallel</u>

Amalgamated Association of Iron and Steel -Workers Strike!

Pittsburgh - July 1892 - Labor strife continues to take its toll of lives in Pennsylvania. Carnegie Steel's Homestead plant outside Pittsburgh has been struck by Iron and Steelworkers refusing to take a pay cut. Carnegie's tough general manager, Henry Clay Frick, seeing a golden opportunity to smash the union, locks up the plant and hires 300 Pinkerton detectives who specialize in guarding plants. The guards' arrival in boats is met by armed workers waiting for them. Four thousand infuriated steelworkers and 300 Pinkertons are left to fight it out. Before hostilities end thirteen hours later, three guards and seven workers are dead and scores seriously injured. Governor Robert Pattison orders out 4,000 National Guardsmen to restore order. The influx of troops breaks the strike after twenty weeks.

STATE PAYS OUT MORE THAN 2 MILLION DOLLARS IN MILITIA AND OTHER COSTS

"AN ENORMOUS SUM TO BE PAID FOR THE GRATIFICATION OF MR. FRICK'S DESIRE TO GET RID OF UNIONS."

Pittsburgh Gazette – 1892

... Alexander Berkman, a Russian-born anarchist, provided a sensational sidelight to the strike. Furious at Frick's use of strikebreakers, he decided to kill the man. While Frick sat in his office talking with a friend, Berkman shot him. But the steel company manager was only wounded. Berkman spent 13 years in prison and was released and deported on the very day that Frick died of natural causes.

STEEL COMPANY LOSES $250,000 BECAUSE OF STRIKE

STEELWORKERS LOSE $850,000 IN LOST WAGES

THE BLACK HUSSARS

PART II

COSSACKS AND HUSSARS

THE BLACK HUSSARS

... from the microfiche ...

"REMEMBER THE MAINE –TO HELL WITH SPAIN"

Havana   February 15, 1898 -   The battleship U.S.S. Maine destroyed by explosion.   260 of the 350 officers and men on board killed.   The whole country thrills with war fever.   Teddy Roosevelt to organize "Rough Riders."

1898 - April —War begins

      May — Battle of Manila Bay

          July — Battle of San Juan Hill

             December —That *"Splendid Little War"* ends

"Oh bury me not on the lone prairie
They heeded not his dying prayer
They buried him there on the lone prairie
In a little box just six by three
And his bones now rot on the lone prairie"

As 1899 came to a close, editors reviewed the century just passing.   The 19th Century, observed the *New York Times*, *" ...had been marked by greater progress in all that pertains to the material well-being and enlightenment of mankind than all the previous centuries of the race; and the political, social, and moral advancement has been hardly less striking."*

FILIPINOS REVOLT AGAINST AMERICAN RULE

"It was that emancipated race
That was charging up the hill
Up to where them insurrectos
Was afightin' fit to kill

And the Captain bold of Company B
Was afightin' in the lead
Just like a trueborn soldier he
Of them bullets took no heed

There's been many a good man murdered in the Philippines
Lies sleeping in some lonesome grave."

NATION GREETS CENTURY'S DAWN!

BUSINESS GREETS NEW CENTURY

LABOR GREETS NEW CENTURY

NOISE GREETS NEW CENTURY

SOCIETY GIRLS SHOCKED: DANCED WITH DETECTIVES

"It is to be a wild night of worship at the feet of Bacchus. One entertainment hall has been the scene of a promiscuous "kissing bee." Girls are dancing on the tables and pledge New Year's bedlam until daylight."

MCKINLEY RE-ELECTED PRESIDENT
Teddy Roosevelt is Vice President

In responding to the toast, "The Twentieth Century," Senator Albert J. Beveridge said: *"The Twentieth Century will be American. American thought will dominate it. American progress will give it color and direction. American deeds will make it illustrious. Civilization will never lose its hold on Shanghai. Civilization will never depart from Hong Kong. The gates of Peking will never again be closed to the methods of modern man. The regeneration of the world, physical as well as moral, has begun, and revolutions never move backward."*

Boxer Rebellion in China
U.S. Troops Relieve Peking from Boxer Uprising

MCKINLEY ASSASSINATED!

ROOSEVELT MOVES INTO WHITE HOUSE

Miners at the turn of the century as they prepared to go to work. Note the oil burning headlamps; a frequent cause of explosions.

Courtesy Applied Arts Publishing

The Mine Below

"This is the fourth day we have been down here. That is what I think, but our watches stopped. I have been waiting in the dark because we have been eating the wax from our safety lamps. I have also eaten a plug of tobacco, some bark and some of my shoe. I could only chew it. I hope you can read this. I am not afraid to die. Oh Holy Virgin have mercy on me. I think my time has come. You know what my property is. We worked for it together and it is all yours. This is my will and you must keep it. You have been a good wife. May the Holy Virgin guard you. I hope this reaches you sometime and you can read it. It has been very quiet down here and I wonder what has become of our comrades. Goodbye until heaven can bring us together." **Dos Passos, _The 42nd Parallel_**

6.

THE BLACK HOLE OF JOHNSTOWN –
MORE THAN 100 KILLED –
DISASTER BARELY NOTICED BY NATION

The Cambria Iron Company, which was later to become the Cambria Steel Company then Bethlehem Steel, was founded in Johnstown, Pennsylvania in the 1850s. It was among the nation's first large-scale iron and steel manufacturers. The company grew rapidly because of technological innovations, the availability of raw materials, and the town's proximity to railroads. The raw material included coal for the blast furnaces. Cambria Iron owned coal mines, including the Rolling Mill Mine that was located on a hillside just across the Stoney Creek River from the city's downtown area.

At eleven o'clock in the morning on July 10, 1902, an explosion ripped through the Rolling Mill Mine and killed 114 men; most of them Polish, Slovak and Croatian immigrants. The disaster was practically ignored in most of the state and nation as media attention was mainly focused on the Great Anthracite strike on the other side of the state. And, because of the difficulty in organizing the immigrant miners in the soft coal regions, the union also sloughed off the tragedy. John Mitchell, president of the United Mineworkers, speaking in Wilkes-Barre, made only one reference to the Johnstown tragedy. *"If mining companies would exercise more care in protecting the lives of their men in the mines, instead of trying to reduce the cost of production, the occupation of a miner would not be so hazardous."*

As rescue workers entered the Rolling Mill mine, local reporters and thousands of panic-stricken relatives, friends of the entombed miners, and townspeople gathered around Powell Stackhouse, the President of the Cambria Steel Company. Stackhouse issued a statement saying there was no *"...list of names of the trapped miners because they were known only by check"* — a metal tag pinned to the shirt of each miner which served to identify him. *"The only way their names would ever be known,"* Stackhouse

41

said, is *"if the bodies are recovered in time for identification and the families send their names to us."*

It was later learned that the explosion itself killed only seven of the miners. The rest died from "after-damp," a poisonous gas, mostly carbon monoxide, which forms after a mine explosion.

At the turn of the century Johnstown was a city of 36,000 persons and more than 7,000 of them were foreign born. The Cambria Steel Company was the city's largest employer with some 12,000 men working in its mills and mines. The company was also the largest employer of immigrant labor. In 1873, Cambria Steel successfully broke a mine strike and from then on it hired only non-union workers and fired any man who spoke about unionization. The immigrants were at first willing to work in non-union mines because most of them had no money after getting to America. To survive they had to accept work immediately and without questioning wages or working conditions.

Miners going down into the mine shafts more than a thousand feet below the surface. This is a double track slope meaning a car loaded with coal is coming up one side while the miners on their way to work go down the other side. Many miners were killed in these cars when they stood up and had their heads crushed against the overhead timers.
(Courtesy of Applied Arts Publishing)

Almost all the immigrants worked as pick miners, a job that required a man to lie on his back for hours at a time, digging the coal by hand. The Rolling Mill mine operated ten hours a day, six days a week and the miners were paid 33 cents a ton for the coal they picked and shoveled into the coal cars. Each miner could produce about three tons of coal a day. That meant they earned about a dollar a day, six dollars a week, or approximately $24 a month, if they worked six days a week, four weeks a month. They were paid, in cash, twice a month, but they seldom saw their full earnings because the company would deduct the cost of their picks and shovels and, in Johnstown, the Cambria Steel miners often had to supply their own timber to hold up the mine's ceiling.

There was one other deduction from their paychecks. The Cambria Steel Company operated a mutual fund and every employee had to pay one dollar a month into this fund. Under the program, the company agreed to pay $1,000 to each employee who met death at work or on the way to or from work. The money was to be distributed to the heirs of the deceased worker. All the victims of the Rolling Mill explosion were enrolled in this insurance program.

In addition to working long, arduous and wearisome hours beneath the ground, the miners also lived in constant fear of explosions, poisonous gases, cave-ins, and other mishaps that could kill or maim. *

The Polish and Slovak immigrants had no hope of improving their employment status. Positions of authority were reserved for native born men, or English-speaking western European immigrants who had lived in the United States for many years and had received their citizenship. All the foremen and bosses in the Rolling Mill mine were earlier immigrants of English and Welsh descent who generally regarded the newer immigrants as inferior and beneath them.

The foreigners in Johnstown, just as in other cities, almost always lived in their own ethnic communities, mingling only with their own nationality. By sticking together, they could share the language and religion

---

*The author's great-grandfather was killed in this mine in 1901 when he was struck on the head by a falling beam.

43

of their native countries. This gave them a sense of security and helped them adjust to a different way of life. Housing, for the most part, was a two-story frame dwelling with two rooms, generally about 12 by 12 feet, on each floor. None of the houses had bathrooms or toilets and an outhouse ten or fifteen feet at the back of the home was universally used. One of the rooms on the first floor was used as a kitchen, dining room and living room for the family. The other first floor room was the bedroom for the family. The second floor rooms were rented out to immigrants who were either bachelors or men who had left their families behind in the old country until they could be sent for or until the men returned home. The usual price paid by these boarders was two to three dollars a month and that included lodging, heat, light, cooking, and washing. Sometimes there were as many as twenty men living in these two upstairs rooms. One boarding house lost 15 of its boarders in the Rolling Mill mine explosion.

The Slavic immigrants were devout Roman Catholics, and from the pennies they earned, they built beautiful churches in their communities. The city school system had no special programs for the immigrant children, consequently, the church, with the priest and nuns serving as teachers, assumed the responsibility for educating the young.

Most of the Rolling Mill Mine victims were members of three Catholic churches — St. Mary's, St. Stephen's, and the newly constructed St. Casimir's Polish Roman Catholic Church. Father Deminski, the priest at St. Casimir's, told the press, *"Over forty members of my church were killed in the disaster in the mine. Most of these men were my best parishioners, being thrifty, provident, God-fearing men who were pillars of strength to the congregation."*

In the Slavic household the husband was the undisputed head of the family. The husband went to the mines and worked and the wife remained at home to do all the cleaning, laundry and cooking for the family and the boarders. Children usually quit school at an early age; the girls to help with the housework and the boys went into the mines to do the same work as their fathers. All members of the family were expected to make a contribution and the wages earned by the immigrant child were turned over to the parents.

The native born population of Johnstown looked upon the immigrants with indifference, ignorance and prejudices, calling them "bo-hunks," or "hunkies." A disparaging letter sent to the daily newspaper after the explosion was not only perfectly acceptable and printed, but the Johnstown Tribune seemed to apologize for offending the non-Slavish employees of the mine. The letter, written by an Anglo-Saxon miner, complained that the newspaper insulted the "American" miners. It read, in part: " ...*the display in the window of the Tribune office of the two dinner buckets found in the Rolling Mill mine, with their contents, is not pleasing to the miners in this city who are American citizens as compared to those who are foreigners. We do not object to the display of the buckets, but the exposure of their contents seems to be a reflection on the fare enjoyed by all those who work in the mines. How the Slavs are accustomed to eating dry bread and a piece of bologna, but the Welsh, Americans and English folks employed in the mines make excellent wages, the most of them, and are able to enjoy an abundance of substantial, wholesome food...*

Signed, A miner

The Tribune printed the miner's letter and then added an explanation immediately following it as to why they showed the empty buckets. *"The contents of the dinner buckets were exposed in the... window display with the purpose of showing first, that the men had not eaten their noon meal when the disaster occurred; that the buckets, food and all, were found, just as represented in the 'The Tribune's' news columns, by the reporter who went through the mine... and to give an idea of the statement that a trail of dinner buckets marked the flight of the dying men from the mine. Far be it from 'The Tribune' to give even the slightest ground for anyone to think that an aspersion on a noble class of men was intended.*

- Editor."

It is not quite clear who the "noble class of men" were.

Then there was the matter of distributing relief funds, together with more than $3,000 found on the 114 bodies of the Rolling Mill victims.

THE BLACK HUSSARS

(These men had little faith in banks and kept all their savings on their person). Mayor John Pendry, facing conflicting claims regarding the beneficiaries of the money found on the bodies, came to the conclusion that: *"those foreigners may have depths of sympathy unknown to us, but they certainly show a desire for money that is not suggestive of sorrow."*

And a prominent physician attending a meeting called to consider offers of aid from other cities, believed that such contributions were not necessary: *"I know a majority of the families who lost a member,"* he said, *"who are now in better financial condition than before his death... Hundreds of them are only waiting for the insurance to be paid them to go to the old country, where they can live for the remainder of their lives in opulence."*

The immigrant in Johnstown, as in other cities, was despised and viewed as a transient who stole jobs from native born Americans, then returned to his own country. In fact, between thirty and sixty percent of the Polish immigrants to the United States did return to Europe. Few of them became naturalized. Of the 83 Polish and Slovak miners killed at Rolling Mill, only two of them were American citizens.

An inquest was held and a mine inspector testified the mining of deep coal *"...is the most hazardous occupation short of war. A spark or a flame may have caused the explosion. Based on our investigation, ventilation was sufficient even though fresh air had to travel down several hundred feet and then circulate through six miles of tunnels and cross tunnels. Yet, a boy and his pony could have knocked down one piece of canvas and disrupted the flow of air. These are 'fiery' coal fields, that are particularly given to the accumulation of explosive gases. Then there is the coal itself. Coal dust that lingers in a tunnel atmosphere and reddens the miner's eye and blackens his lung is, in proper ratio to oxygen, almost as explosive as gunpowder. One might ask how any man would take a chance on working in subterranean chambers so filled with known and unknown dangers? How could any father kiss his children good-by in the morning knowing that by evening they might be orphans? But this is an emotional and shortsighted response. To close the mines would bring industry to a halt.*

Mills would lie empty, trains would stand and rust in their yards, ships would idle at their docks. A single human error, one breach of orders, may well have been to blame for this disaster."

Four days after the explosion the mine resumed normal operations. Damage to the mine itself was $1,000, and other immigrants soon replaced the miners who had been killed. The inquest found, with no proof, that a miner in violation of company rules used an open lamp in a section of the mine known to be dangerously gaseous. The inquest also found the Cambria Steel Company to be innocent of any acts of negligence.

The union leader felt cocky. It was 1908 and the UMW was getting stronger every year. This wildcat strike in Somerset County would be over in a few more days, but the mine owners had to be taught a lesson. The two hundred men he was leading down the dirt road to the colliery, the only road that led to the mine site, were carrying pick handles and shovels as their weapons. They would not blow up the colliery. That would be foolish, it would keep them out of work too long, but they would tear it up enough to show the mine bosses that this union local could not be intimidated by the Sheriff and his few deputies guarding the company property. Midway down the hill one single horseman, a State Trooper, rode onto the road and halted. The "Black Hussars" had been in existence just three short years, but they already had a formidable reputation. The mob paused. The leader growled at the Trooper

"Out of the road, Cossack. We're going to the mine and you're in the way. Beat it!" This brought a cheer from his two hundred followers.

"You'll have to turn back," the Trooper said. "You are forbidden to go down this road."

"Hahh!" the leader sneered, "you can't stop all of us." The crowd began yelling and waving their weapons at the State Policeman.

The Trooper placed his hand on his holster and calmly replied. "Maybe I can't stop all of you," he said to the leader, "but you will be the first to die."

The union boss was stunned. "But you would be tried for murder!" "Perhaps," the trooper replied, "But you won't be at the trial."

Without another word, the leader turned away and started back up the road followed by the grumbling mob.

... from the microfiche ...

"I met my love in the Alamo
When the moon was on the rise
Her beauty quite bedimmed its light
So radiant were her eyes"

A grand parade has been proposed in which President Roosevelt shall ride so that he can be seen by the citizens. At the head will be a caged bear recently captured after killing a dozen dogs and injuring several men. The bear will be turned loose and given an hour's start for the hills then the packs will be set on the trail and President Roosevelt and the guides will follow in pursuit.

1905

BLOODY SUNDAY IN MOSCOW

CZAR YIELDS TO PEOPLE

"There's a girl in the heart of Maryland
With a heart that belongs to me
And Maryland
Was fairly-land
When she said that mine she'd be"

7.

America the beautiful — Prosperous - Moral - Brave - and, Contented. Anyone living in poverty could only blame it on his own laziness or drunkenness. There were no poor people in America. Prosperity was here for everyone. Or at least that was the myth that endured as the 20th Century entered its third year. The reality, however, was quite different than the myth.

Out of a work force of some thirty million men and women in 1902, more than ten million worked in agriculture. Most of the remaining work force was employed as factory workers, domestic servants, lumberjacks, seamstresses, clerks and miners—oh, yes, and a few doctors, lawyers, politicians, civil servants and teachers. But they were the professional class. The average worker-week was 59 hours and the average pay, including skilled and unskilled workers, was less than $10 a week. 84-hour work-weeks were not uncommon in the steel industry.

Coal miners, about 350,000 in 1902, were, as the saying went, "brought into the world by the company doctor, lived in a company house or hut, were nurtured by the company store ... laid away in the company graveyard." The day began for the men at dawn when they went down into the coal pits where, with picks or explosives, they pried chunks of coal from the seam and shoveled it into an ore car. Boys, as young as seven years old, got their jobs separating stone from coal by claiming to be fourteen, the legal minimum age in the early part of the century. Mine cave-ins and explosions occurred regularly, each killing from a few to scores of men and boys.

A coal miner was not paid by the hour in 1902, but by the ton — a "miner's ton" — which often meant 2700 pounds or more, a source of frustration and wrath among all the miners. Until he heard the whistle in the morning, the miner never knew if he had work that day or not. When the price of coal dropped, the companies would cut back on work to a few days a week. Even in good times families lived on the ragged edge of poverty and life expectancy was short.

THE BLACK HUSSARS

America's total population was 76 million persons and more than ten million of these people were immigrants, mostly from Russia, Ireland, Italy and the Slovakian countries. Even though many young girls and women worked in the sweatshops of the textile industry, the stay-at-home population outnumbered the work force because the mothers in most families, especially the immigrants or first-generation Americans, had eight, ten or twelve children. The men worked outside the home, the women were homemakers. The foreigners held the worst jobs, with the longest hours and the lowest pay, largely because few had a trade and even fewer had a command of English. The situation was ripe for socialism and unions.

Labor unrest was widespread in the industrial and mining communities across the nation. Pennsylvania, more than any other state, was in desperate need of a fair and reliable law enforcement agency to keep the peace during the frequent strikes by immigrants in the coal and steel regions.

Moreover, the rural areas were rife with crime of every description. Aside from the National Guard, pressed into costly service when labor unrest erupted into widespread rioting, and an ineffective sheriff-constable system, the State provided one other agency for the enforcement of law in the coal fields and steel towns; the hated Coal and Iron Police. To make matters worse, it was in the interest of these thugs to stir up violence during any strike and keep tempers hot. It gave them job security of the cruelest kind.

Workers were "hitting the bricks" almost daily in some part of the nation. The biggest strikes, however, in terms of numbers of workers who stayed off the job, took place in Pennsylvania. The state produced much of the nation's coal and most of its steel. As a result, it employed the greatest number of foreign coal miners and steelworkers.

At the turn of the century, the population of Pennsylvania was 6.3 million people. Of these, two and a half million, or about 38 percent, were either foreign born or the children of foreign born parents. The children, at that time, were heavily under the influence of their parents and approached social problems in the same way as their fathers.

Before 1840, mass immigration to the United States was welcome. There was plenty of room and work for all and, besides, the immigrants were from the British Isles and Northeastern Europe. They were of the same ethnic group as the founders of the nation — mostly white Anglo-Saxon Protestants. American policy in the middle of the 19th century, written into law, encouraged immigration in spite of the prejudices aimed at the Irish in the wake of the potato famine. But then the immigrants started to pour in from Russia, eastern and southern Europe. Between 1899 and 1910, 2.3 million immigrants arrived from Italy alone. This situation, described as "alarming," eventually led to the setting of immigration totals.

American business could be "blamed" as much for this mass immigration as the potato famine was to "blame" for the Irish exodus to the United States beginning a half century earlier. Cheap labor was needed in the factories and mines and on the farms. A binding labor-contract system with the immigrants was developed between American businessmen and Italian bureaucrats and opportunists. It was immensely profitable for those who ran it and exploitive to those subjected to it.

Like the "Coffin Ships" that brought the Irish to the United States a half century earlier, the filthy, intolerable conditions on the ships that transported the Italian immigrants is hard to imagine. The city of New York began to charge the ship owners a ten-dollar fee for each dead immigrant aboard when the ship arrived in port. The Captains got around this by making sure all the dead immigrants were buried at sea, even if the ship was just a few hours from port, and then altering the passenger lists to avoid the ten-dollar penalty levied by the city.

Richard Gambino wrote in *Blood of my Blood:* "At first the labor movement resented the Italians as cheap labor threatening their uphill attempts to organize the American worker. And, indeed, attempts were made by American companies to use the early Italian immigrants as 'union busters.'" A Congressional Commission in 1907 reported that "strike after strike in the Pennsylvania coal fields" in the late 1800s "was smashed when employers brought in Slavic, Hungarian, and Italian labor."

As each wave of immigrants descended on American shores, they had to struggle with predecessors for a decent foothold. Additionally, for one reason or other, they were often in trouble with the law. Their frequent turbulent and violent activities became a matter of deep concern to those who wanted to see law and order prevail.

In 1902, thousands of coal miners walked off their jobs in the anthracite coal fields of Eastern Pennsylvania. This strike was the genesis of the first state police force in the nation. (PA State Police Col., ret.) Philip Conti wrote: *"Many sheriffs' deputies and labor rioters were killed in skirmishes at Lattimer that year, and the 'Great Anthracite Coal Strike,' as it was to become known later, was more than Pennsylvania and the nation could endure because of its own characteristics and its spill-over effect upon the nation."*

For the first time, the critical need for a state police force was being given more than lip service.

Miners at the turn of the century became the "shock troops of American labor," winning 160 of 260 disputes in one year, primarily in the soft coal regions of the State. As much as the coal barons despised the unions and constantly tried to smash them, their profits and the nation itself depended on coal, and the mines could not be shut down too long. It was prudent on occasion to reach a settlement with the miners. Nevertheless in the hard coal regions of eastern Pennsylvania, union successes were seldom and few.

But in spite of setbacks, the United Mineworkers of America was a growing union in contrast to the steelworkers who had been losing members, especially after J.P. Morgan formed U.S. Steel in 1901 and the union overreached in its demands. The steel union, forced to capitulate to management's terms, was left in a shambles.

It was a different story with the miners union that welcomed to membership almost anyone who had anything to do with coal mining. With some recent successes in the soft coal fields in western Pennsylvania, West Virginia and Kentucky, the union's chief, John Mitchell, was ready to take on the hard-coal operators in eastern Pennsylvania. The anthracite mine owners were fewer and stronger than the soft-coal owners were. It was a problem for Mitchell and, to add to the union's predicament, the anthracite miners were less united than those in the soft-coal fields. Catholic members traditionally fought with Protestants, native born Americans fought with immigrants, and immigrants fought with one another.

Mitchell visited every hard-coal town in the state to sign up recruits. Between native-born Americans and immigrants he drew no distinction: "The coal you dig isn't Slavish or Polish or Italian or Irish coal," he insisted, "it's coal!"

His persuasiveness was overpowering and, on May 12, 1902, 150,000 miners left the pits in the hard coal region of the state and Pennsylvania faced one of the worst industrial strikes in the nation's history.

The strike lasted a year and a half, until October 23, 1903. When it finally ended through the intervention of President Theodore Roosevelt, it had destroyed the equilibrium of the State. Many lives were lost and a bitter harvest was sowed. It cost the striking miners $25,000,000 in lost wages; it cost the coal companies more than $46,000,000 in production; it cost the transportation companies $28,000,000 in freight losses; and it penalized the nation with a coal shortage and a hike in the price of anthracite coal. On top of everything else, in order to maintain law and order, it forced the State to call out its entire Division of National Guard at a cost of $1,000,000.

In addition to the cost in hard dollars, there was another hardship brought on by the strike that was borne not only by miners and consumers, but by young men derailed from their careers. Nearly nine thousand guardsmen, citizen soldiers, were suddenly yanked from their jobs and homes. The Adjutant General, in a subsequent report, said: *"Troops had been on duty for one hundred and five days continuously. To call men away from their varied professions, business, and employment, without warning or opportunity to make arrangements for so prolonged an absence, required a great sacrifice on the part of many officers and men... nor was ever duty more exacting."*

THE BLACK HUSSARS

At the first session of the President's commission, Roosevelt invited Mitchell and the leading coal operators to meet in Washington. The union leader, represented by Clarence Darrow, said his men would accept whatever a government-appointed board of arbitration ruled, provided the coal operators would agree to do likewise. But the operators said they would not deal with *"a set of outlaws,"* and the meeting adjourned without result. Afterward, Teddy Roosevelt said of one of the coal mine owners, George Baer: *"If it wasn't for the high office I hold, I would have taken him by the seat of his breeches and the nape of the neck and chucked him out of that window."* Other conferences were soon held, however, including one on J.P. Morgan's yacht, and the coal operators agreed to accept federal arbitration.

Five months later, the arbitrators rendered their decision: a ten percent increase in pay, a nine-hour day for most of the workers, the right of miners to select the check weighmen to oversee the weighing of coal, and a conciliation board to be formed for hearing workers' grievances. This was less than Mitchell demanded, but more than he had been ready to settle for.

The Presidential Commission had worked diligently throughout the winter of 1902-03, listening to the testimony and complaints of all three sides in the great, bitter strike — those of the union men, the non-union men, and the mine owners. It recognized the justice of many of the complaints from miners, but also the need by the coal operators to hire armed guards — the Coal and Iron Police — to protect their collieries. Under existing conditions, it said, the necessity of the Coal and Iron Police must continue even though it worked injustice and contained the seed of great evil.

Although the leaders of the mineworkers union who began the strike had exhorted their followers to make it a peaceful walkout, the local union bosses paid little or no attention to those orders. The commission branded the history of the strike as "stained with a record of bloodshed and violence; cruel, cowardly and uncivilized behavior."

Finally, the commission weighed the evidence as to the worth of the existing machinery for the preservation of the laws and the peace of the

Commonwealth of Pennsylvania and discovered that the existing law enforcement machinery had practically no worth at all. The State itself stood guilty. It evaded its duty to enforce its own laws with its own hand, at all times and seasons, to protect the people in the full enjoyment of peace and safety.

"Peace and order," the commission declared, *"should be maintained at any cost, but should be maintained by regularly appointed and responsible officers at the expense of the public."*

Instead, the State had turned its duty into a shabby piece of merchandise and sold it into private hands, the steel companies and mine owners who used the law to form the Coal and Iron Police.

President Roosevelt's Anthracite Strike Commission, at the very first of its general recommendations, issued a clear call for legislative action to create a proper executive arm to enforce the laws with impartiality for the good of all men and the honor of the State. In short, the commission was calling for the creation of some kind of state police force.

It was while William A. Stone was Governor of Pennsylvania (1899-1903) that the "Great Anthracite Strike" took place. On January 6, 1903, Governor Stone gave his final "State of the State" address to the general assembly in Harrisburg and talked at length about the strike, calling it a major catastrophe. *"The strike of the miners ... in the anthracite coal regions was probably the most important and far-reaching event of its kind that ever occurred in the State,"*

Stone then went on to explain the sequence of riotous and uncontrollable incidents that prompted his decision to call up the National Guard for strike duty. *"The National Guard served for 105 days,"* he said, *"the longest period during the last fifty years ... except for the industrial disturbances at Homestead near Pittsburgh."*

Stone then referred to his message to the general assembly in 1901 when he sought a compulsory arbitration law to settle difficulties between employers and employees. Noting that the legislators had ignored his recommendations at that time, he warned the lawmakers upon his departure that significant action needed to be taken to end these costly disruptions.

8.

PENNYPACKER

Samuel Whitaker Pennypacker was the new Governor of Pennsylvania when Roosevelt's Commission at last made its findings and recommendations public. Pennypacker was a man of intense devotion to ideals and the courage to defend his principles against all comers. Like many educated and industrious men in those days, Pennypacker wore a number of hats in his lifetime. He had been a member of the bar of Pennsylvania for forty years and a judge for fourteen years. The newly elected governor had a logical and deliberative mind and was a student and writer of the state's history. He came from an old Pennsylvania German family, what some people still call "Pennsylvania Dutch" ... and was a conservative Republican, as most of the Keystone State's governors were for forty years before and after Pennypacker.

More than anything else, however; more than his judicial posts, his law firm, his writing of history, Governor Pennypacker took pride in being a farmer. It was in his blood, his tradition, and he believed fervently that it was unjust that the State was unable to protect its country people who always offered the State its strongest support. Others had felt this way before Pennypacker became governor, but in a conservative old society like Pennsylvania's, there was much consideration and passive resistance to changing the "old ways."

When the President's Anthracite Strike Commission had recommended the creation of a state police force, although they didn't call it that and might have had something entirely different in mind, Governor Pennypacker acted immediately even though the legislature would not meet until the following year. (In those days, they met only on alternate years.)

The farmer-Governor needed no time to make up his mind. A few years later he would tell the story of how it all got started. Using his own words: *"In the year 1903, when I assumed the office of Chief Executive of the State, I found myself thereby invested with supreme executive authority. I found that no power existed to interfere with me in my duty to enforce the laws of the State, and that, by the same token, no conditions could release me from my duty to do so. I then looked up to see what instruments I possessed wherewithal to accomplish this bounded obligation — what instruments on whose loyalty and obedience I could truly rely. And I perceived three such instruments — my private secretary, a very small man, my woman stenographer, and the janitor ...So, I made the State Police."*

Before his term as Governor, Pennypacker had brooded for years about the plight of the country dweller who, in effect, had no police protection. And he brooded, too, on the evil of the Coal and Iron Police and their growing power.

Then, when the great Anthracite Strike hit the state, the scandal of the Coal and Iron Police burst into the public mind once again. At the time Pennypacker took office, there were five thousand of these strange and hybrid officers who held commissions that had no time limit. They were rapidly becoming a private army and constituted a blight upon the State.

"The exercise of the power to enforce its laws," Pennypacker said, *"is one of the most important functions of the Commonwealth, and should be performed by the State only. If the State does not herself see to it that her peace is maintained she fails in her first duty."* Pennypacker meant every word he said.

The President's Commission could only recommend a course of action which included the idea that some sort of state police force might be formed to alleviate the violence and length of labor disputes, not to mention dismantling the hated Coal and Iron Police. But only the Chief Executive of the State could act on, or ignore, the Commission's recommendations. Pennypacker wasted no time in making his views known and was determined to see a strong, impartial State Police Force come into being for the "honor of his beloved Pennsylvania." He swore to himself that the coming legislature would not dissolve until his vision was realized.

In spite of his determination, getting the State Legislature to form a new department in the face of all the inherent political plums and the drain on the treasury, wouldn't be an easy task. A lot of resistance, active and passive, cropped up as soon as his wishes became known. For one thing, the unions with its large membership of foreigners had a legitimate fear of any kind of "State Police." Many of those union members had fled to America to get away from the Russian Cossacks, the Austrian-Hungarian Hussars, and other forms of European-style police who were really no more than soldiers dressed in fancy uniforms and serving at the pleasure of a king. They carried swords as well as guns and used them, quite often unjustly, to put down any kind of dissent.

The "strange bedfellows" of the immigrants in opposition to the creation of a State Police Force were the farmers and other conservative citizens who had been in the state for generations. They didn't like the idea of creating another bureaucracy and the taxes that would go with it. But Pennypacker persisted. On May 2, 1905, he signed the Act that would give Pennsylvania the first State Police Force in the nation.

———————————

... from the microfiche ...

The American scene, from the turn of the century until the United States entered World War I, was a period that began with a feeling of almost smug satisfaction with the way things were. People laughed at the "horseless carriage" and dismissed the Wright brothers' first airplane as some sort of trickery. The very rich believed themselves the beneficiaries of Darwin's principle of natural selection, which absolved them of any concern — much less responsibility — for the tragic plight of exploited labor.

... from the classifieds ...

"... GIVE US ONE THOUSAND RANGERS"

Mention the Pennsylvania State Police as the first State Police Force in the nation, even to many natives of the State, and in surprise they'll respond, *"I didn't know that."* Make that statement to people in other states, and they'll likely say, *"What about the Texas Rangers?"*

In 1835, the Texas general council formally organized the Rangers and assigned them the sole task of defending the frontier against Indians. The Rangers learned the Indian skills of horsemanship, woodcraft and direction finding.

When Texas gained its independence in 1836, it faced a Mexican and Indian danger on a 1,000 mile frontier. With a population of 400,000, it could not afford a standing army. Texas required a fighting force that was small and inexpensive, available in time of need but inactive when not needed. The Texas Rangers, without uniforms, drill, or regular pay, met these requirements. They served as a mobile and efficient frontier defense organization. Like Cincinnatus, they left their plows when needed and returned to them when the danger passed.

After Texas joined the Union in 1845, the Rangers continued to play a major role in frontier defense. During the Mexican War (1846-1848), they performed valuable service as scouts and guerrilla fighters with the

59

American armies in Mexico. The federal government soon established forts along the Texas frontier and garrisoned them with regular troops, but Texans still placed their faith in the Rangers. Sam Houston once said in the U.S. Senate:

> *"Give us one thousand Rangers, and we will be responsible for the defense of our frontier ... we ask no regular troops; withdraw them if you please. I ask this not through any unkindness to them, but because they have not the efficiency for frontier service."*

The Rangers were disbanded several times over the years, usually because of the politics of the governor in office. When Governor Miriam "Ma" Ferguson took office in 1933, Adjutant General W.W. Sterling resigned his office and forty Rangers left with him. It looked like the Texas Rangers were going into the ashcan of history. Under Governor Ferguson, Ranger commissions were easy to come by, *"and not all those handed a Silver Star were men whose character was worthy of the honor."* Ferguson appointed 2,300 Special Rangers, and a few of those were even ex-convicts.

In 1935 the Texas Senate created an agency which would operate under a three-member Public Safety Commission. The Texas Rangers were transferred from the Adjutant General's Department and the Highway Patrol would be moved from the Highway Department to form a single state police force. Under the new Department of Public Safety (DPS), the Rangers would consist of 36 men.

In their early years, as part of the DPS, the Rangers were given a Colt .45 and a lever action .30 caliber rifle by the state. Rangers had to provide their own car, horse and saddle, although the DPS issued horse trailers and paid automobile mileage. In 1994, the Ranger force was increased to 103 men. Although they operate without a special uniform, you can spot a Texas Ranger by his western boots and hat, badge and guns.

Prior to the Industrial Revolution, police departments were, for the most part, non-existent. England had its system of county sheriffs dating to the first millennium that was continued by the conquering Normans after 1066. This arrangement, which in the 19th and 20th centuries frequently grew into a political plum, was adopted by Colonial America and continues in most states to this day.

One reason why paid, professional police systems were not adopted was because of a reluctance in both England and the United States to organize any law enforcement group with uniforms out of concern that it made them look too much like the king's army. Nevertheless, Sir Robert Peel created the first professional police department for the city of London in 1829, a body of trained and paid policemen for day and night duty.

The first police force in the United States was in Boston in 1838. Six men were paid to stand watch during the day, but the nights were still left to unpaid watchmen or to men, hired by wealthy citizens, who served only their employers, much like the Coal and Iron Police. The large influx of immigrants to the United States, however, gave rise to wide spread clashes between foreigners and native-born Americans. Major riots in New York City was the impetus for the State Legislature in 1844 to pass a law establishing an 800-man police department in the city to deal primarily with the battles between the immigrants and the native-born. Other cities soon organized police departments following the pattern of New York. Preventing or stopping riots by the use of these city policemen worked for minor skirmishes between a few people, but failed to bring major rioting to a halt. When full-scale battles broke out, state officials had no choice but to call up their organized militia, a costly action to be avoided if at all possible.

One major riot — the New York City draft riots of 1863 — has been described as "the most serious challenge to law and order in American history." The City policemen, who had been organized for nearly twenty years, were completely overwhelmed. Federal officials in Washington found it necessary to recall military units from combat zones to the unlikely battlefield of Manhattan. It has been conjectured that the number of dead in the draft riots exceeded by far the anticipated number of draftees who would have been killed in Civil War service had the New Yorkers responded lawfully to the call to arms.

In Pennsylvania in the 19th century, professional police forces were organized only in Philadelphia and Pittsburgh. All the other counties in the state were served by an ineffective sheriff-constable system. The constable system, incidentally, was established as a form of state police in Massachusetts and other New England states in the mid-nineteenth century.

This system was adequate, Katherine Mayo said, *"when Pennsylvania's rural population came of generations of law-revering stock. But all this changed... in part through an influx of foreign immigration ... greater in numbers and less in understanding... to our laws. Looking about them, these men saw no gendarmerie, no carabinieri, no uniformed patrol upon the road."*

Northumberland County Sheriff Dan Sweeney called the Pennsylvania State Police barracks yesterday (December 2, 1909) pleading for assistance to restore peace to the troubled community of Mount Carmel. The sheriff was told help would be sent to the riot scene immediately. This information was passed onto the mayor who went to the outskirts of the town and waited for the arrival of the State Police. Within a very short time, one mounted trooper came riding up the road. "Where are the rest of the men?" the mayor exclaimed in horror.

"Rest of the men?" The puzzled trooper replied. "There was only one riot reported."

(A similar version of this apocryphal anecdote is attributed to a Texas Ranger)

9.

CAPTAIN GROOME

The Act that created the Department of State Police was deliberately loosely drawn to allow the first commander a great deal of leeway as he put together something that had never been tried before. It was a brief and simple document designed for an entirely new and experimental organization. Its success or failure rested entirely upon the shoulders of whoever was to be selected as the head of the Department. Governor Pennypacker noted that *"A loose law gives a good man rein the quicker to make good, while it gives the bad man rope the quicker to hang himself and so have done with him."*

Newspapers around the nation were editorially hailing the experiment, suggesting their own states should consider similar statewide police forces. The *Chicago Tribune* mirrored the thoughts of other editors when it wrote: *"...The problem of preventing and securing the punishment of crime in the rural districts of the United States has yet to be solved. The counties have peace officers in their sheriffs and the townships in their constables, but the way in which these officials perform their duties in most places leaves much to be desired...The situation is usually much aggravated when crime takes such a form as a lynching or a riotous strike. The best remedy is probably such a measure as that which has been adopted in Pennsylvania ... If property is to be made secure and life is to be made safe throughout the rural districts of the United States, the State constabulary system will probably have to be generally adopted. Pennsylvania's experiment with it should be highly interesting and instructive."*

Meanwhile, Pennsylvanians and their newspapers were anxiously waiting to see whom the Governor would appoint as the head of the new Department. This could be a real political plum with more than two hundred jobs at stake. The names of men for appointment to fill the post of superintendent for the new department poured into the Governor's office for consideration. But Pennypacker didn't reveal his thoughts to anyone.

There was a wall of silence surrounding the Chief Executive's office for two months.

Finally, on July 1, 1905, the Governor announced his choice. To the shock and dismay of politicians, and to the delight of newspaper editorialists, Pennypacker offered the appointment of Superintendent of State Police not to a friend of the powerful "political machine," nor to someone who could bring in votes, nor to someone who had ever served him. The man he chose was of no use to Pennypacker's party or to him personally, but rather a complete outsider. The farmer-Governor offered the Superintendence of the State Police to Captain John C. Groome, commander of the First City Troop of Philadelphia. First City Troop was part of the National Guard and should not to be confused with a militia organization known as the State Fencibles that would be humiliated by mobs a few years after the State Police were formed.

The Governor's enemies were stunned. There was nothing they could publicly say about the choice. The press was elated: "Political Machine Gets Rap," "Machine Hard Hit," "Out of Politics." All over the State, urban and rural newspapers praised Pennypacker's choice. The *Harrisburg Telegraph* said: *"It is fortunate that the experiment... is to be carried out under the supervision of an officer of the character and caliber of John C. Groome... to no better or safer hands could the work of organizing the force be committed and his choice removes any misgivings as to the real aim of the new department."*

In Pittsburgh the *Gazette* noted that Groome *"...has the knowledge of military organization and practice, understands the work to be done, and will bring intelligence and integrity to the task. He is not a politician."*

But not all the newspapers were happy with the selection of Groome. Some, whose publishers were deeply involved in partisan politics, felt the "plum" should have fallen under their influence. One small urban paper even complained that Groome was a "gentleman."

It appeared that Governor Pennypacker had selected a paragon to head the newly created State Police Force. Groome had a reputation, both as a citizen and as a military figure that approached perfection. He had been a member of the Pennsylvania National Guard, "First Troop, Philadelphia City Cavalry," since 1881. This was the oldest military organization with continuous service in the United States. Formed in 1774, First Troop's original complement was made up of twenty-eight gentlemen who in times of peace had ridden to hounds, hunted and fenced together. It equipped itself as a mounted Company, and under the name "Philadelphia Troop of Light Horse," offered its services to George Washington. From that time until the end of the Revolutionary War, the command practically lived in the saddle. At the end of the war, in signing its dismissal, General Washington thanked them *"...for the many essential services which they have rendered to this country and to me personally, during the course of this severe campaign. Tho' composed of Gentlemen of Fortune, they have shewn a noble example of discipline and subordination, and in several actions have shewn a Spirit of Bravery which will ever do Honor to them, and will ever be gratefully remembered by me."*

The City Troop maintained its standards without a break since its formation in the 18th century right into the 20th century. It fought in every one of the nation's wars and did its duty through periods of riots and disorder.

Groome was elected to command of City Troop in 1896. Two years later, at the outbreak of war with Spain, he and every man in his command volunteered to enter Federal service, taking the oath just seven days after war was declared. Once again, the Troop distinguished itself.

(A few years later, Groome would again serve with distinction as a Colonel under General "Black Jack" Pershing, Commander of American troops in World War I.)

Upon Pennypacker's announcement that he would appoint Groome as the first Superintendent of the Pennsylvania State Police, the *Philadelphia Inquirer* said: *"If Captain Groome will bring his State Constabulary up to the efficiency of the First City Troop, the State can hardly ask more of him."*

65

THE BLACK HUSSARS

Groome   **Lumb**

Captain John C. Groome, the first superintendent of the Pennsylvania State Police and his assistant, (later the second Superintendent of the Force) Captain George F. Lumb

Everyone assumed that Groome would accept the appointment with no hesitation. Groome turned down the job. Pennypacker was convinced, however, that the Philadelphia "Blue Blood" was the only person who could make the Pennsylvania State Police an organization that would not only be successful, but a Force in which the Governor could be proud. Using all his persuasive powers, Pennypacker finally convinced Groome to take the job. But Groome accepted only on the stipulation that one rigid condition had to be met: *"If I take the task of organizing the new State Police,"* he said, *"there will be no place in the Force for political henchmen or ward politicians, no toleration of wire-pulling in any shape. If, or when, I cannot run it on this plane, I shall turn the commission back to the Governor to dispose of as he pleases."*

Lynn Adams, the man who eventually succeeded Groome and George Lumb as superintendent of the Force, wrote in his memoirs: *"...at the time, many thought that Captain Groome was merely paying lip service to a high ideal. In an atmosphere so permeated with politics as*

Pennsylvania's, they incorrectly presupposed that the new Force would quickly become a tool of the party in power. As the years rolled by, however, and the non-political record of performance grew and grew, all doubt faded that a new kind of police force had, in actuality, been created.... It was this kind of promise (independence from politics) that attracted men of high caliber to the force from the very beginning."

Governor Pennypacker was delighted with Groome's response and the conditions he laid down. It was exactly what the Governor wanted and expected. He had resolved that the Pennsylvania State Police should be his monument in the State's history; whatever else might have feet of clay this must stand firm — this must be founded on solid rock. Groome was the man to perform the task.

John Charles Groome was born in Philadelphia in 1862, a descendent of an English sailor who settled in Maryland in 1650. Groome's ancestors included Colonel John Connelly who fought with the Artillery during the Revolutionary War. An outstanding Polo player, Groome was a member of the Radnor Hunt Club, the Philadelphia Country Club, the Philadelphia Club, Rabbit Club, Army and Navy Club of New York, Pennsylvania's Historical Society, Military Order of Foreign Wars, and Military Order of the Spanish-American War. It might sound like Groome was a society dandy, but nothing could be further from the truth. In 1892 - 1894 he drove public road coaches to places as far away as New York, and was on cavalry teams that won contests in the United States and Europe. He was also a successful businessman. A very handsome young man in all respects, Groome married Agnes Roberts in 1884. They had three children who were grown when he formed the State Police at the age of 43.

With the exception of his World War I service, when he was Provost Marshal of the American Expedition Force in France, Groome was in complete charge of the State Police until 1920. Then he petitioned to be relieved of his $3,000 a year Superintendent's post so that he could return to his business. When he died in 1930 at the age of 68, the flags at the various barracks of the State Police Force were flown at half-staff for thirty days and the members of the Force wore black crepe on their uniforms.

THE BLACK HUSSARS

As soon as word got out that Groome was to be the Superintendent, a flood of applications for places on the Force poured into Harrisburg. As usual, many of the applicants tried to assure their acceptance by going through Senators and other political offices. Groome would have no part of this political pressure. First he announced that due to the enormous amount of work necessary to perfect the organization, no appointments to the Force would be made until the fall. Then, using the press to get the word out, he reasserted his initial position that: *"... politics will not figure in the Department, and the men I shall select will get their appointments entirely on their fitness and not through political influence."*

When the Act creating a State Police Force was signed into law, every detail of organization was left entirely to the discretion of the Superintendent. This meant Groome would be responsible for the selection of manpower, for framing the rules, for setting the specific duties of the Force, for making regulations under which it should operate, for determining its equipment and arms, uniforms, for the decision as to whether it should be mounted or not, for the location of troop headquarters and for setting the rules of the examination of applicants.

Groome knew that he was breaking new ground that was vitally important not only to Pennsylvania, but to the entire nation. Years later he said, *"I proceeded very carefully. There was no precedent, nothing to pattern by, and the matter was as new to me as to everybody else."*

Although moving prudently, Groome wasted no time in getting the new organization off the ground. The first thing he did was make a careful study of the criminal statistics in each region of the State to determine where the State Police would be most needed. Next he studied the records of the world's various law enforcement agencies — The Northwest Mounted Police, the Germans, the Texas Rangers, Australian, and Irish police. After comparing them all, he reached a tentative conclusion that conditions and geography in Ireland more closely paralleled Pennsylvania than any of the other territories. Ireland and Pennsylvania are practically the same size — forty-five thousand square miles.

Groome headed off to Ireland to study its Police Force. He found much of interest to help his work, but the Irish Force consisted of ten thousand men to police a country the same size as Pennsylvania. And that number did not include the Dublin Police Force. The new Superintendent of the Pennsylvania State Police had two hundred and twenty-eight men to be assigned to him compared to the thousands in Ireland. Although Philadelphia, Pittsburgh and some of the other large cities in the State had their own police, it still left a vast territory to be patrolled and protected by a few men.

Groome returned home in late September to report to the Governor. In the meantime, Dr. Francis D. Patterson, the examining surgeon of the Force-to-be, had been conducting physical examination of the men who wanted to join up. It was a diverse group — cowboys from the west, athletes just out of universities, farmers, officers of the National Guard, militia men and men who had served honorably in the regular army and navy. Over one thousand applicants had filled out the necessary forms as the first step to join the force. This all happened within a month of the Governor signing the Act to create the Pennsylvania State Police. Dr. Patterson than arranged to tour the State and give physical examinations at fifteen different locations in an effort to avoid unnecessary financial hardship on the applicants. The examinations exceeded by a large margin those given by the regular army. When Patterson finished his tour, only two hundred and fifty applicants remained from the more than one thousand who applied.

The next step was a mental test to be carried out on November 4, 1905 in Harrisburg, Pittsburgh and Philadelphia. One hundred and ninety-three men made it through this phase of testing. In addition, their records of conduct and morality were thoroughly examined. These one hundred and ninety-three men became the original personnel of the Pennsylvania State Police Force. They came from twenty-two different States and eleven foreign countries. Thirty-five percent of the Force in 1905-06 was not native Pennsylvanian. Ninety percent of them had served from one to three enlistments in the regular army and had not only honorable discharges, but also commendations.

Next came the selection of officers. The four captains and four lieutenants were picked from the cream of the State National Guard. Of the twenty sergeants, fifteen had been non-commissioned officers in the regular army and the other five were State Guardsmen. None of the appointments had the slightest hint of political favor. The people and the press were pleasantly pleased with the absence of politics and the tough standards set in the selection of the personnel for the Force. In fact, they were so delighted that a competition cropped up between the various counties around the state vying to have one of the four State Police Barracks located in their communities. Town leaders offered inducements to Groome in an effort to snare one of the four Troops, but to no avail. Groome listened to them, but had only one criterion for placing the Troops — areas where the necessity was greatest.

After due consideration, he placed one Troop at Greensburg, Westmoreland County, in the southwestern part of the State; a second Troop to the north in Punxsutawny in Jefferson County; a third Troop in Wyoming, Luzerne County in the northeast and the fourth Troop at Reading, Berks County, located in the southeastern part of the State.

None of the Troops were quartered within a town, emphasizing that the State Police had no intention to supersede any existing police officers. This meant that barracks had to be found outside of town limits, creating another logistic problem for Superintendent Groome. As he later described the situation; *"Finding it was impossible to secure a building in the vicinity that would be large enough to accommodate an entire Troop, I was compelled to rent buildings that would be as close as possible to the purpose for which they would be used, and then make the necessary additions and alterations."*

At the same time that Groome was selecting sites and approving barracks, he was assigning the men to their Troops, ordering uniforms and equipment, and buying horses. Two hundred and thirty mounts, selected in accordance with U.S. Cavalry specifications, were purchased from a ranch near Fort Worth, Texas, shipped by train to Pittsburgh, and distributed to the four Troops.

10.

DAWN OF THE BLACK HUSSARS

Gathered into four Troops, the men who would soon be known as "The Black Hussars," as well as several other sobriquets, assembled at their quarters in four sections of the State. A few of them had served together in the regular army but, for the most part, they were strangers to each other, arriving at their new homes from different states and different countries including England, Ireland, Germany, Austria, and South Africa. Before serving in the American military, many of them fought in the armies of their own countries, some of them on different sides such as in the Boer War. One common goal they all shared, however, was to be the best police officers on earth. Their initial inspiration came from their superintendent. Groome told them individually and in small groups: *"You are now the State Police Force. It is your duty,"* he said, *"to make the Pennsylvania State Police Force the finest thing in the world."*

He then gave them some cardinal rules that must be obeyed at all times, and a philosophy of conduct: *"It is possible for a man to be a gentleman as well as a policeman"* — *"I expect you to treat elderly persons, women, and children at all times with the greatest consideration"* — *"When once you start after a man you must get him"* — *"In making an arrest you may use no force beyond the minimum necessary."*

Some ten years later, one of the original members of the Black Hussars recalled the early days in these words: *"Men came onto the Force with no other idea than that of making it the best in existence. Those who did not feel that way did not long survive. And through and above all the stiff training that each of us needed and got, ran the paramount influence of the Superintendent's personality. It was that one man's mind, felt straight through the Force, that set the standard for us all. It underlay every rule or teaching. It was, and is, a silent, sleepless, inevitable call upon all of the very best that a man can give."*

Groome had an innate talent to get people to do what he wanted them to do, and to like doing it. More important, he had the ability to get these same men to not do what he thought they should not do, and believe that not doing it was reasonable and logical.

The Act that created the State Police Force did not permit the purchase of property to house the men and their horses. Consequently, it was necessary to lease what would become their first barracks and it was a logistical nightmare to find housing that would accommodate fifty-five men as well as stables for their horses. As Groome pointed out later, it was practically impossible to locate and lease such quarters in the small towns where they would set up the Troops.

The men of "A" Troop, stationed near Greensburg, found a large unfinished, uninhabitable house they could rent. It also had an unfinished stable, that is, some uprights and cross-timbers were in place. The first thing the Troopers did when they detrained at Greensburg on a cold, gray winter day, was hunt down some rooms where they could board. Then they immediately started to help with the construction of their future home, digging trenches for drains and sewers, working on grading and scores of other jobs. The chores were endless. One detail of ten men under the supervision of a carpenter, worked on the stable, putting up walls over the frame and building bins, chutes and stalls for the horses. The Superintendent decreed that every man in the Force should be mounted, and the horses were to arrive at any time.

This presented a problem that was solved with an ingenuity and perseverance the Black Hussars would employ throughout their early years. A train unloaded the horses at Pittsburgh, some thirty-five miles away, while the men were still working on the stable. Nervous and unstrung by the long train trip from their Texas home, the horses had to be bedded down, but the stable wasn't yet ready. The only thing available was at a racetrack on top of a steep hill a mile and a half from the town. It could be reached only by a dirt road covered alternately with snow and mud. The troopers put the horses at the track, then climbed the hill four times each day to take care of their mounts while the stable was being completed.

From the very start, the horses of the Pennsylvania State Police were bought in Texas and in accordance with the Superintendent's exact specifications. The horses were small — rarely over fifteen hands — wiry, agile, light feeders, and chosen for endurance. The slight training they had in Texas bore little relation to the work for which they had to be broken. The highest price ever paid for these horses, up until 1916, was $165 each delivered in Pittsburgh.

At the beginning the only practical way thousands of miles of rural area could be patrolled was with mounted troopers. Other forms of transportation at the time were limited to trains, trolley cars, or walking. But even as the automobile began to make headway as a means of transportation, the Black Hussars continued to rely on their horses for decades. A few years after the beginning of the State Police, Groome was asked whether it was really desirable that all troopers should use horses on their patrols.

"The Force," he answered, *"must always be a mounted force, for character. The prestige of a man on horseback is psychological, rooted in the depths of the human mind. To disregard this fundamental fact would be an extravagant folly. For riot duty, experience has proved the mount to be indispensable; the theory that a mounted man cannot make an arrest to advantage is amateur's nonsense. Again, for observation patrol, among a variety of definite uses, no other means of locomotion equals the horse. But for certain emergencies,"* Groome conceded, "the possession of one or two high-powered automobiles and *a few motorcycles would undoubtedly increase the efficiency of each Troop."* The engine-driven "mount" was still years away. Up until 1916, "A" Troop was the only one of the four Troops to possess a car.

All the troopers could ride, but only a few understood the training of the horses. It was up to these skilled equestrians to teach the rest. Men and horses together practiced every day to mount and be mounted at a gallop; to ride double and to bear a double burden; to hang by a horse's neck and to let your man hang by your neck — all these things and more the man and horse learned together.

When the "barracks" were ready, the troopers applied themselves to learning criminal law. Books were supplemented with lectures given by specialists. Police officials and detectives came to the barracks to talk about their own specialties and to throw practical light on the academic studies of the men. The "classroom" training ran side by side with the daily horse drills, revolver practice and instruction in emergency crafts.

The experience of "A" Troop at Greensburg was pretty much the same for the other Troops. "B" Troop near Wilkes-Barre had to rent office space from the Kulp Detective Agency for ten dollars a month. "C" Troop near Reading, like "A" Troop, made out the best they could with temporary lodgings until their barracks could be prepared. The men of "D" Troop at Punxsutawney were initially quartered at a hotel until their leased barracks could be made habitable. It was an old fair exhibition building whose flimsy structure was unable to keep out the winter wind and rain. But regardless of their quarters and the time and work they had to put into making them suitable for Spartan living conditions, everybody went through the same drills, the same classroom studies, and the same hardships.

This training and renovation of barracks and stables took place in the winter of 1905-06. By spring, the uniforms and equipment had arrived at the various Troop headquarters. The Superintendent himself designed the outfits with one thought in mind. They had to be durable, practical, and maintain permanent neatness. The uniform consisted of a military tunic and riding britches of a very dark gray whipcord. It looked black. There were black pigskin puttees, black boots, nickel strap spurs, a reinforced black helmet with a black leather chinstrap, and black horsehide gauntlets. On either side of the tunic collar was a permanently riveted nickel letter almost an inch high, which was the letter of the Troop. A quarter of an inch from each letter was a nickel number of the same size. This was the personal number of the individual trooper. The numbers could be read from a great distance and they could not be removed without destroying the coat. Its purpose was to furnish a positive means of identifying the trooper in the event anyone wished to make a complaint against a specific man. The idea of the number came from Major Groome and was later copied by the New York City and Philadelphia police departments. The front of the helmet displayed a large "badge" with the words "Pennsylvania State Police Force"

Not only were the members of the Pennsylvania State Police required to be well groomed at all times, but their horses, too, were to be in the best of shape. Note the long riot batons hanging from the saddles.

in nickel circling the badge. The center of the badge depicted the State's arms in black. A cartridge belt and holster was worn on the outside of the tunic.

The officers' uniforms were identical to those of the men with the exception of the collar ornamentation. Officers did not wear a number or Troop letter on their collars, but instead had the State's arms. Also issued to the men were an army fatigue cap, a campaign hat, a rubber coat, an overcoat for mounted wear, and a stable suit.

Like the uniforms, the same thought and consideration went into the choice of weapons selected for the troopers. Each man was equipped with a 38-caliber Colt revolver, a billy club; a long hickory baton carried on the saddle of his horse, and a Springfield carbine. The rifle was not for daily use but kept for special emergencies. On March 1, 1906, the troopers had been fully equipped and went into the field on active duty. But not all of those men who had been initially selected for the Force the previous fall were still around. The discipline and hard work had taken its toll. Several men had resigned. A few others were asked to leave when, under working conditions, it was found they lacked the judgment, steadiness and moral fiber demanded by the Superintendent. Not all those who began with a Captain's rank met Groome's perception of the "finest thing in the world." Not every young, athletic man was cut out for rising at dawn to care for his horse and having a line of conduct marked out that left no margin for self-indulgence.

These were not weak or bad men, but simply men who could not quite measure up to the standards of the new Force. Not for a moment did these dismissals or resignations give Groome pause to perhaps consider making the standards a shade less rigid (There was no "political correctness" or "affirmative action" programs in those days). There would be more men to take their place; men who could measure up to criteria set by the Superintendent, and the sooner the shortcomings of the men were discovered, the better for the Force and the rest of the troopers.

A few years after the Force had been formed; a Captain of the Black Hussars was asked the difference between the Pennsylvania State Police and the Canadian Northwest Mounted Police. *"The difference,"* he answered, *"is that the Mounties have a guardhouse, and we have none. With us, the best man goes on his first lapse of conduct. We know no such thing as a second offense."* This is borne out by the attrition rate of troopers that, in some years during their first decade in the field, reached fifty percent.

It was Groome's plan to cover the entire state with the small force. But some areas of the state needed more attention than others. The central region, for example, was mainly a farming area with an old, homogeneous and sparse population. Although there was crime in this area as elsewhere, it was far lower in magnitude and violence than in the steel and coal mining regions in the eastern and western parts of the state with their large immigrant populations.

Economics, customs, and working conditions were the primary causes of lawlessness among immigrants. Labor disputes between management and workers were a constant source of violence. After the State Police came onto the scene, the scope and severity of rioting in labor disputes diminished dramatically. But that didn't end crime in mining communities among the immigrants themselves. This was particularly true in the Italian communities where an organization called the Black Hand - a genesis of the Mafia - exploited fellow immigrants from Sicily and Italy. The Black Hand was, unlike the early days of the Mollie McGuires, purely a criminal organization without any pretense of bettering the lives of the workers. The members of the Black Hand were Italians preying on other Italians.

Another economic basis for violence that kept the Black Hussars busy in the large immigrant areas was, ironically, too much money. The wages paid the miners and steelworkers were meager, but far more than what they could have ever scraped together in their homelands. This cash, coupled with the harsh working conditions they endured, was an incentive to indulge in heavy drinking whenever they emerged from the mines and steel mills at the end of their shifts, or on the one day a week they got off. The flow of alcohol often led to bitter fights, knifings, the beating of wives and children and, not infrequently, to small "riots" between Slavs and Italians, Italians and Irish, and even among themselves.

Robbery, murder, rape, and arson happened everywhere in the State, but hardly on the scale that it occurred in the steel and mining regions. At feasts, christenings and balls, the immigrants were given to heavy and prolonged drinking bouts that often ended in wild and murderous disorder. The practice of the sheriffs and constables was to let them alone in their ugly moods — to let them fight out their brawls undisturbed.

"So long as they confine their sanguinary conflicts to their immediate associates," one rural newspaper said, *"the general public will have small cause to complain."* It was not held seemly *"that any worthy, honest man should imperil life or limb by thwarting a knave in his knavery."*

The State Troopers had an entirely different outlook and approach to these mini-riots. Whenever they were summoned or came across them while on patrol, they immediately squashed them. The Black Hussars soon established a reputation for putting down disturbances even-handily and promptly as well as taking into custody criminal suspects that local law authorities too often ignored or were too afraid to arrest.

Shortly after the new State Police Force became active, the public discovered the troopers to be, as a Wilkes-Barre newspaper put it, *"clean, lithe, athletic, agile men,"* whose mere presence at the scene of trouble had a calming effect. The Troopers demonstrated at the outset of their patrols that they could and did serenely handle any type of lawlessness from murder to mob violence.

Nonetheless, labor-management violence appeared to be the *"raison d'être"* of the State Police. These lithe young men had the opportunity from the very beginning of their active patrols to prove their ability and resolve, for 1906 brought Pennsylvania an abundance of industrial disturbances. Both the eastern and western parts of the state were ready to erupt into labor violence. The newly formed State Police seemed to be everywhere at once, and they demonstrably smothered the sparks of passion and uproar before they could erupt into a burning fury. There was little doubt in anyone's mind that had there been no State Police, the National Guard would have been needed and pressed into service on more than one occasion that eventful year.

During the great anthracite strike of 1902, the entire eastern region of the State was flaming out of control before the Guard was called. By contrast, in 1906, when hundreds of workers in the Punxsutawney district began a riot that the sheriff could not control, a small detachment of Black Hussars from "D" Troop arrived on the scene with their horses and batons and quickly restored peace. "D" Troop had demonstrated its character and courage to the citizens early on and the rioters knew what to expect if they defied the Black Cavalry. What once would have been a riotous situation needing a mobilization of Guardsmen and the shedding of blood, "D" Troop's mere appearance stilled the disorder and averted bloodshed. No force was needed; simply the calming effect of the early presence of recognized power.

On the other side of the State a short time after the Punxsutawney business, "C" Troop put down an upheaval in Lebanon County. The New York Evening Post described the incident: *"At the Cornwall ore-banks ...*

78

five hundred foreigners became angry because they could not persuade the men keeping the fires to quit work. They assaulted several inoffensive workmen and chased away the sheriff's deputies. The sheriff telephoned the State Police Barracks for aid: 'Send your whole force,' he urged. 'These rioters are desperate.' A sergeant and ten men from the barracks were dispatched ... no sooner had they arrived than the smallest Trooper in the Force shoved his way boldly into the crowd of angry men and grabbed a big foreigner who had pulled a gun. The prisoner showed fight and his comrades offered to help him. The Trooper swung his stick just once, the big fellow dropped, and the crowd ran like sheep.

"...Two thousand armed men to one troublesome town was the Militia's ratio for pacification. By the ethics of the Black Hussars, a sergeant and ten men are expected to handle such a situation. The mounted constable enforces the law. He must be absolutely fearless. If he shows the white feather once, his usefulness is over and the Force has no place for him."

12.

BOSTON PATCH

On the morning of April 4, 1906, trouble broke out at the Fernwood Colliery, not too far from Wilkes-Barre in eastern Pennsylvania. There was no strike at the coal mine, but a group of Italian immigrants were furious that non-union workers - "scabs" - worked at the colliery. They tried to make the non-union men walk off their jobs. The Italians occupied a community called "Boston Patch," a small settlement on a hill overlooking the colliery that was about two hundred yards away, an area that had a reputation as being a hangout for roughnecks and bandits. It was one of those areas the local peace officers avoided at all cost. The place was simply too rough.

The mob in Boston Patch went about its effort of persuasion — getting the workers to walk off the job — by shooting at the colliery. This went on all night and a handful of local policemen were helpless in their attempts to stop the gunfire. Actually, they were afraid of the armed mob and stayed away from it. By morning bullets splintered the roofs and walls of the colliery, but, luckily, no one had yet been killed. The law officers at the scene put a call in to Captain John Loftus of "B" Troop asking him for help.

Loftus immediately dispatched Sergeant Ray Garwood and two troopers to the scene of what was on the verge of becoming a riot or, more accurately, an armed attack on the colliery and the possibility of severe beatings to the men who worked there. When Garwood arrived on the scene, he was greeted by a mob of several hundred blustering immigrants. When he told the angry men to disperse, their leaders aimed revolvers at Garwood. Swinging their batons, Garwood and his men charged their horses into the mob, straight at the leaders who turned and fled into the houses of Boston Patch. Garwood then phoned the barracks for more assistance for he intended to clean up the "Patch." Captain Loftus sent Sergeant Tom Dimon with ten more Troopers.

The two sergeants and twelve men then proceeded to go through

Boston Patch like a hot poker through snow. The troopers kicked in doors at houses where mob members were hiding and dragged them out into the street. Before the morning was over, the Black Hussars had confiscated an arsenal of firearms that had been concealed in beds, chimneys and walls. The leaders of the mob were arrested and the disturbance came to an end. But it wasn't the end for Sergeant Dimon and three of his men.

The United Mine Workers Union swore out warrants for the arrest of the troopers. They were charged with trespassing and disorderly conduct for entering the houses of Italian residents and searching for weapons. The four State Policemen surrendered themselves for arrest and in due course were acquitted of the charges. The Philadelphia *Telegraph* noted that the arrests of the Troopers was outrageous, but would probably, in the long run, be entirely beneficial. As the newspaper put it:

"The action of the men was prompt, unflinching, and eminently successful. That they should be subjected to arrest for doing their duty... seems like a discouraging miscarriage of justice, but if it serves to establish the legal authority of the Constabulary on a firm basis and enforces respect for the personnel of the force, the test may possibly serve a good purpose. It should be the part of all good citizens to see that the vindication of the men has their unqualified approval and support."

The UMW, however, wasn't going to give up easily. At a local union convention in Clearfield, Pennsylvania, the union passed a resolution demanding repeal of the State Police Act and the dismantling of the Force. They also called on all miners to support those legislative candidates who would pledge themselves to support a repeal of the law that created the State Police. This led the Philadelphia *Press* to exclaim:

"It is just this sort of thing that is injuring the cause of the mine workers. In years past the Coal and Iron police were denounced in unmeasured terms; the police of every city and borough and the sheriff of every county that organized and armed a posse to protect life and property in the coal regions was condemned as the arch enemy of organized labor. In other words, any individual invested with police power is the enemy of the striker, no matter what position he may hold ... the resolution of the United Mine Work-

ers District No. 2 may be the forerunner of similar resolutions from other bodies. But the State Constabulary has come to stay."

Early on the press called them the State Constabulary so often that many people believed it was their official name. It wasn't. Hussars, Cossacks, Constabulary were colorful nick names which immediately helped to enhance their frightful reputation for crushing outbreaks of civil disobedience. To a rioter or criminal accustomed to cowing a local sheriff or town constable, there was no question that the Black Hussars could be frightening or intimidating. The fact is that in their exchanges with ordinary citizens, and especially with women and children, they were polite and willing to go to any lengths to protect them. Nor did they in any way resemble "Cossacks." They were simply an arm of the Department of State Police with the official title: **State Police Force of Pennsylvania.** And as tough as they were when they needed to be in order to enforce the law and carry out their duty, they also were considerate and helpful and adherence to the firm dictum of their commander. Otherwise, they didn't last.

At the start, the four Troops totaling slightly more than two hundred men were assembled in a relatively brief period. There was not much time to dig too deeply into their records and backgrounds, but it didn't take long for Groome to recognize the ones whose records on paper far exceeded their practical ability. He soon demoted some of the originally appointed captains, lieutenants and sergeants, or discharged them from the Force as unsuitable to meet its high standards. But within a year after its formation, and with a long list of applicants trying to get on the Force, the recruiting was done much more stringently. When a man asked for an appointment to the State Police, he was told to fill out an application showing his past experience and references. The application was then added to a waiting list while a careful inquiry was instituted into the record of the applicant. If his past record showed the slightest flaw, his name was no longer considered for entry into the Force. If, however, his experience and character were sufficiently good, the man was then summoned to Harrisburg or Philadelphia and put through a rigorous physical examination. Upon passing the physical and a mental test, he was then enlisted and sent to "C"

Troop barracks at Pottsville where he would spend four months as a probationer, unless he was weeded out before his first probationary period was completed.

In Pottsville, the probationer was taught the criminal laws of the State. He also went through a daily grind of mounted and dismounted drill, taught the care of horses, and had instructions with firearms, equipment and the general duties of the Force. The training during these probationary months was deliberately designed to be extremely harsh, and when a man dropped out under the tough conditions, his going was welcomed. There was room on the Force for only the best and most determined men. It was better for all concerned to weed out early those who could not make it as a Trooper. Besides, getting rid of them early saved the Department time and money, both commodities in short supply.

The trainees soon learned that life wouldn't be an easy 12-hour day and then, at bedtime, sleeping through the night like most people. It was more likely he would be turned out of bed at two o'clock in the morning to ride a horse twenty miles in a blizzard for the pleasure of possibly having his head blown off by a drunken lunatic molesting a vacant lot. And most of all, if the probationer had a white feather (cowardice), the sharp eyes of the veteran troopers were almost sure to spot it. If he made it through the first four months of training, he then was assigned to one of the four Troops, but he would not be permitted to go out on an assignment or patrol by himself. There was another long period of fourteen months probation when he always would have to be in the company of a veteran Trooper before he was turned loose on his own.

Promotions were invariably made from the ranks. In 1916, with ten years of experience under his belt, Groome said, *"I have not a captain or lieutenant today who held that position when the Force was formed.*

At that time it was necessary to select what I considered the best-trained men who came before me. Some of those men, in the course of time, did not prove all that I wanted of them. They were not fitted to handle the position and were therefore dropped out. After the original formation, I have never started a man on the Force otherwise than as a private."

83

A group of Black Hussars heading out at daybreak. It is interesting to observe that even at a full gallop the men appear to be at attention – heads held high, left hands on the reins, and right arms straight at their sides.

Of the two hundred and thirty officers and men that composed the Force ten years after its founding, two hundred and twenty-five were honorably discharged soldiers of the regular army. Many of these men had been non-commissioned officers and had served two or three terms of enlistment with the highest recommendations on their discharge papers. In spite of the best previous training and experience in the military, no man was considered thoroughly qualified to be a State Trooper until he had been put through eighteen months of the special training that Troop schooling and the pairing with a veteran Trooper provided.

Punishment for misconduct was governed entirely by court-martial that was conducted by the offender's commanding officer. If the accused proved that the charge against him was incorrect, no record was made of it; if found guilty, the evidence, with the sentence of the court was submitted to the Superintendent who either confirmed or modified it.

"The men all know," Major Groome said, *"that if they behave properly, they can remain on the Force; that if they do not behave properly they*

will be fined or dismissed; that once they are dismissed no power on earth can get them back again, and that if they conducted themselves as they should and fulfill their whole duty no power on earth can procure their dismissal."

In the early years of the Force, there was a continuing "weeding out" of men who were deemed unsuitable. Thirty, fifty, as many as ninety men a year could not meet the demands of the Black Hussars and either resigned or were dismissed. That's a very large percentage for a Force consisting of 230 men. But the rules were rigid and they were never bent. The charges leveled against these men included having liquor in their quarters, asleep on duty, abusing a horse, and *"conduct unbecoming a State Policeman and a gentleman."* It should be noted that, almost without exception, the men who were dismissed were new recruits and that their failures occurred in the early days of their enlistment.

Inasmuch as the Force was experimental, Major Groome decided not to frame a code at its beginning, but rather to depend on regular military discipline, supplemented by general orders issued as developments required. General Order Number 6, issued in 1908, is more than interesting in light of today's principles:

"Any member of this Force known to have used outside influence for the furtherance of his interests will be considered as <u>acknowledging his incompetence</u> and will be dropped from the service."

The first victim of General Order Number 6 was a lieutenant who wanted to fill a vacancy in the rank of Captain. The lieutenant had some clout with a senator and other influential people who wrote to Groome and urged the appointment of their friend. When Groome received the letters he promptly wrote out a dismissal from the service order. The lieutenant not only failed to get the promotion, but also was booted off the Force.

General Order Number 27 was issued in 1909. It reads: *"Any member of the Force who is found guilty of having taken an active interest in politics, or who has endeavored to influence the vote of any other person, either a member of the Force or a private citizen, will be Dishonorably Discharged and fined two weeks' pay."*

THE BLACK HUSSARS

This order, like all the other general orders, meant exactly what it said and was observed to the letter. From the Superintendent down through the ranks, no trooper or officer on the Force could acknowledge the political beliefs of any member of the Force in any way. Politics were strictly taboo to the Pennsylvania State Police.

General Order Number 3 was issued in March of 1907, just two years after the Legislative Act created the Force and one year after the Black Hussars took to the field. This was an order regarding marriage. In the beginning the men were accepted onto the Force without any thought given to their marital status. A few of the men who enlisted in 1905 had wives, but most of them were single. Within a short time there was a rash of weddings and the Superintendent felt the necessity, *"for the good of the service,"* to bring it to a halt. He decreed that *"to maintain the efficiency of the Force, and owing to the fact that married men sleep out of barracks and are not immediately available at all times for service, hereafter any member of the Force getting married will be honorably discharged."*

"I know it seems rather severe," Groom said, *"but marriage will not do for our troopers. In this work minutes count.. Our men must be ready to swing into the saddle at the briefest notice, day or night; and that means barracks life. We do not enlist married men now, and it is unjust that a man may enlist as single, then shortly marry and still remain in the ranks."*

Soon afterward there was a modification made to General Order Number 3. It was amended to allow marriage in due time: after having served two terms of enlistment, or four years, a trooper could marry if his Captain approved. It was determined that after four years of service a trooper would fully realize how much time he would have to give to his family and what the risks were in his job. Also, his third enlistment would result in a slight increase in pay which would help to meet the expenses of a family at a time when wives were not part of the job market but rather fulfilled the role of homemakers.

As mentioned, one of the obligatory drills of every Troop was in the use of firearms and meant a lot of target practice with pistols. Within a few years after being organized, the Pennsylvania State Police revolver team held the United States Revolver Association's Medal and the Winans Trophy. The Winans Trophy is the award for team shooting and a sergeant and three privates on the State Police team were the best-recorded revolver shots in the world. This practice paid off many times for all the troopers. One particular incident involving the Greensburg barracks was brief and dramatic.

It seems that on January 10, 1914, a report came into "A" Troop's barracks from the County Coroner, H.A. McMurray, that " ...*on this night...an insane man had assaulted him and attempted to kill him with a knife, and had since barricaded himself in a house, in Youngstown, and was defying local authorities.*"

Sergeant John Graham and Private Robert Snyder rushed to the scene and, according to their report, "...*found the insane man barricaded in a small dark room, furious, and armed with a large butcher knife. Owing to the position he had taken, it was impossible to overcome him by direct methods. So, while Sgt. Graham held the ray of his flashlight on the man, Private Snyder shot the knife from his hand with his service revolver. It was then possible to close with him without any particular injury to officers or the prisoner.*" So read the report from the Troop "A" files.

The "classroom" training also paid off in a big way. The state laws were pounded into the heads of the recruits. When they finally did go out on their own to enforce the law, they could be certain that they themselves were not breaking it. Another state law enforcement agency served to vividly remind them of what could happen if arrests were not made with the utmost care. The bizarre events that took place are a farce and an injustice to the victims who believed they were doing their duty as State Agents. Yet, according to the law, they were in the wrong. This is what happened as it was outlined in the Chief Game Protector's Annual Report for 1911:

"*In this year, in Armstrong County, two special wardens set out under official direction to seize a number of shotguns in the possession of aliens. In Pennsylvania, it may be recalled, aliens are forbidden by law to*

TARGET PRACTICE

In their early years the members of the Pennsylvania State Police won top honors both nationally and worldwide in pistol shooting competition.

have such weapons. The guns were properly seized, without the use of violence, and duly forwarded to the office of the Game Commission; so also were the fines collected therewith. The wardens then had fulfilled their simple duty and no wrong had been done to anyone. Nevertheless, those wardens were promptly arrested for burglary, robbery, extortion, and several other charges..." due to a faulty search warrant.

The wardens spent a few weeks in jail and then they were hit with some stiff fines. After paying the fines, the plight of the game wardens got worse. It seems that when the wardens were ordered to confiscate the guns, they went to a Justice of the Peace, the usual procedure for getting a search warrant. But the J.P issued one warrant to cover several houses. This is against the law, but the game wardens didn't know it and they acted on the strength of the justices flawed knowledge of the law. The jury found the game wardens guilty and the Court refused to consider the circumstances of the case; that the men were under commission and bond from the Game Commission; that they were enforcing established laws by appointed means, and that the only real fault lay in the legal ignorance of the Justice of the Peace. Unmoved, the Court sentenced the wardens to pay fines, with the alternative of one hundred days' imprisonment in the State Workhouse.

Then things really got rough on the wardens. This was 1911 and the prisons didn't have TV sets, telephones, menus for meal selection, or weight rooms. The "workhouse" meant exactly what it said. The Wardens had six indictments against them, but they were convicted on only one. The attorneys for the aliens paid the wardens a visit in prison and told them, in effect, *"You're going to have to pay back our clients all the money you took from them; also the costs; also the full value of the guns; also our fees as attorneys. Then we will see that the remaining indictments are quashed. Otherwise, no sooner are these hundred days done than you shall be imprisoned again, and yet again, 'til you forget the face of the sun."*

The record shows the wardens did pay hundreds of dollars, a princely sum at the time, in fines, costs, damages to the aliens, and fees to the attorneys. The legal profession hasn't changed much in a hundred years. The State Fisheries Commissioner, in his report a year later, noted that *"... in ninety-nine cases out of a hundred, an ordinary Justice of the Peace fails completely when taken before a court of record on certiorari."*

The State Police, on the other hand, were scrupulously trained in the law and made their arrests and cases unerringly. *"We have not one man,"* Major Groome was pleased to announce, *"who has been on the Force for two years who cannot present a case before a Justice of the Peace and present the proper evidence. For that reason, our total number of convictions in proportion to our total arrests is very large. We have averaged eighty to ninety percent of convictions to the arrests made. This is only rendered possible by the fact that the men know when they have the right to make an arrest, when a crime has been committed, what constitutes proper evidence, and how to present that evidence in bringing the case before the Justice.*"

The State Police preferred to have a case nol-prossed rather than bring it into court without sufficient evidence. They believed cases tried without securing a conviction were a waste of time and cost the State money without effecting any good result.

In the Troop school, along with the general teaching of the law the troopers were trained to never bolster up a case under any circumstances, and never, whatever the circumstances of a case, either to show or to be inwardly influenced by personal hostility toward the prisoner. This stolidity, both in court and in the field, added to the imposing reputation of the Black Hussars, a reputation that stuck with the Pennsylvania State Police long after the horses and "Bobby" hats were gone.

PART III

PHILLY FLIPS
AT SIGHT OF STATE POLICE

THE BLACK HUSSARS

... from the microfiche...

EARTHQUAKE DESTROYS SAN FRANCISCO
700 DEAD FROM FIRES AND DYNAMITE

San Francisco - April, 1906 "700 people are dead and four and a half square miles of buildings have been destroyed by an earthquake that broke water mains hampering firemen and soldiers from the Presidio in their efforts to put out fires. Dynamite was used to destroy entire blocks of buildings to contain the fires. The re-building of the city has already begun."

Provisional Governor and U.S. Troops
Re-establish Order in Cuba

PRISONER TWICE TRIES SUICIDE
"I got no money. I no more have any friends"

That is the lament of a Croatian immigrant, forty year old Joe Cozilla, who on Saturday night tried twice to commit suicide at the Johnstown Central Police Station. In each try he was unsuccessful, but a deep cut on the head speaks eloquently of the sincerity of his attempts at self-destruction.

Cozilla's first attempt on his life was spectacular. Crawling to the top of the iron railing around the upper tier of cells at the police station he dived headlong to the cement floor twenty feet below alighting on his head. Prisoners who rushed to his side found a nasty scalp wound but the fellow seemed to have retained his consciousness, and, after his injury was dressed, he was locked in a cell. Some time later he attempted to hang himself with his belt and was suspended from the bars of his cell when attention was attracted to him. Again he was unsuccessful and he has since been divested of every article which might be employed by him in his desire to end his life. When asked why he attempted suicide, Cozilla declared that, 'them fellows tried to kill him.' He was laboring under great excitement and seemed possessed of the idea that he had escaped a terrible death at the hands of his enemies.

Johnstown Tribune, 1906

... from the classifieds ...

The Driver Boy was usually 14 years old and wore an oil-burning lamp on his head and rubber boots because he walked in the ditch, and he carried a braided leather whip called a "black snake." The mules were kept in stables underground until an Act of the Legislature in 1965 made it illegal to keep animals in the mine. Most of the drivers pampered the animals feeding them sweets and teaching them how to chew tobacco.

"My sweetheart's the mule in the mines,
I drive her without reigns or lines,
On the bumper I sit
I chew and I spit
All over my sweetheart's behind."

Each Driver Boy sang his own version of this song   -   some unsuitable for polite ears.

Mule Driver

Like most Driver Boys, this lad is about 14 years old. The boys wore rubber boots because they had to walk in a ditch. They carried a braided leather whip called a "black snake" to "inspire" the mules.

12.

TOUGH KIDS

The 20th century was well underway and only seventeen states had set a minimum age of 14 for children working in factories. The minimum age was a joke in the coal mines. Many of the young boys working in the mines never reached the age of 14 and, if they did, their bodies had been through hell. The "breaker boys," few of them over 12, most of them 8, 9, 10, and 11 years old, labored six days a week for the mining companies for a few pieces of silver. Age was no barrier to getting a job. Physical size determined fitness; desire and the ability to work got them their jobs. The breaker boss, who did the hiring and firing, determined who would work and who would not.

These children would sit in position near the chutes facing the endless river of coal in tedious and backbreaking work for nine hours a day. They would reach into the passing coal and remove slate, rock, slag and other impurities. Every mine had anywhere from 150 to 300 of these boys literally working their fingers raw, suffering from painful "red tops," the term used to describe their fingers when the outer skin was rubbed off to expose the red flesh underneath.

HELPING THEIR FAMILIES TO SURVIVE

Breaker boys at the turn of the century working at the Eagle Hill Colliery owned by the
Philadelphia & Reading Coal Co. Some of them are less than ten years old; none are older than
twelve. The slate picker boss always carried a stick and often used it on the boys.
(Courtesy of Applied Arts Publishing)

The breaker boys' boss would stand over them with a stick to probe
chutes when they became clogged and to probe any boy who made him
angry. If the boy went too far with his antics, he was fired and told to "beat
it."

The first coal breakers were built in the 1850's and were "dry
breakers," that is, water wasn't used to clean the coal. The high, wooden
"sky scrapers" were filled with coal dust that penetrated the lungs of the
boys and covered them with so much soot they were hardly recognizable to
each other.

By the end of the 19th century, water was used to wash the coal
and, to a small degree, it eliminated some of the danger and dirt. A series of
steam pipes under the seats where the boys sat kept them warm in winter,
but the machinery in the building was so loud it was impossible to hear a
spoken word. If a boy had to relieve himself, he would raise his arm above

97

his head and the breaker boss would point to the door with his stick then shake it vigorously meaning the boy shouldn't take too long.

Since they couldn't hear each other talking, the boys had a series of gestures they would use including drawing their fingers and thumbs over the jaw two or three times which meant, "Where is the boss?" Because of fire danger, the boys were not allowed to smoke tobacco, so they learned to chew it which, among other things, helped to overcome the taste of the coal dust penetrating every pore in their bodies.

The biggest moment in the life of a breaker boy was his first payday. Excused from his post for a few minutes, he would go to the paymaster's window and receive his wages in a brown envelope — 35 cents a day for a nine-hour day. One dollar silver cartwheels were the currency. The money was taken home by the boy and handed to his mother. The affection on her face was his greatest reward, but often he was allowed to keep as much as twenty-five cents to use as spending money for the next two weeks. It was a princely sum for a boy in those days. The 25 cents in cash went a long way for two reasons: first of all, they hardly had time to spend it and, second, the purchases they did make - candy, ice cream and tobacco - never exceeded a nickel and most items were one or two pennies.

If the boys made it through childhood they went down into the pits as miners and then died at an early age from black lung disease, assuming they weren't killed in a cave-in or explosion. But many of them never made it into adulthood. They would lose limbs or be killed from unprotected revolving wheels, ropes, belts, scraper lines and machinery. Other graves were filled with their young bodies because of their insatiable curiosity. They had a habit of leaning out of windows in the high wooden structures where they worked. To their young eyes, the view was wonderful, but too often many of them would stretch out too far on a dare or just to see better, and then they would fall to their deaths on the hard ground below.

"You made me what I am today
I hope you're satisfied
You dragged me down and down and down
Until the soul within me died"

THE BLACK HUSSARS

13

BERWIND-WHITE

Spring, 1906. Uniformed and armed, the Pennsylvania State Police were now patrolling the state on horseback and making their presence known in the rural areas and coal towns. Within a week of the brand new law enforcement agency's call to active duty, Troop C was sent to the Cornwall Ore Banks in Lebanon County to restore order at a riotous strike scene. It was during that action that the immigrants in the region began calling the troopers "Black Hussars". In less than a year, their first year as the Force, they would be required to put down more than a dozen major disorders around the state.

The Cornwall Ore Banks disturbance, as mentioned, was dispatched in short order with a show of force that cowed the rioters. In a way, it was much the same story in the soft coal regions of Western Pennsylvania where miners at the Berwind-White Coal Company in Windber went on strike in an effort to unionize the mine. But before the dust of this labor dispute finally settled, people were killed and the immigrants applied another name to the troopers – "Cossacks".

Coal is often found where there have been major uplifts in the land, such as the one that formed the Allegheny Mountains. As a result of this upheaval by nature, southwestern Pennsylvania coal had a dramatic effect on the development of the nation. During the late-nineteenth and early-twentieth centuries, Western Pennsylvania coal fields consistently produced about one-fourth of America's fuel.

A powerful force in Allegheny coal mining was the Berwind-White Coal Mining Company. The company established a central town for its regional offices, Windber, which has remained a viable community to this day. Windber, an anagram of Berwind, was founded in 1897 and quickly became the biggest coal-mining town in the bituminous regions of Southwestern Pennsylvania.

Located in the northern part of Somerset County, just a few miles from Johnstown, Windber was the home and birthplace of Johnny Weissmuller. The son of German immigrants, Weissmuller established more than fifty American and world swimming records in the 1920's and then achieved even greater fame in the 1930's as Tarzan, the most enduring and popular actor to play that role in the movies.

Berwind-White was the area's largest employer and mining coal was the sole reason for Windber's existence and its prosperity. On April 2, 1906, a month after the State Police took the field and just a few weeks after the disturbance at the Cornwall Ore Banks, union organizer Joseph Genter led five thousand miners off their jobs in Windber. The Berwind-White mines were tied up tight. Not a single ore car left any of the mine entrances.

The miners, mostly immigrant Slovaks, Hungarians, Poles and Italians, had a long list of grievances that included not only their wages and working conditions, but the way they were treated in the town itself. At the mine, they were unhappy about the company's weights and weighing system, which they considered to be grossly dishonest. Three thousand pound tons were the rule rather than the exception. In the town, a sore point was the company-owned store where they were forced to buy their food. The autocratic rule of the company was like rubbing salt in the wounds of their pride. Neither American-born miners nor immigrants had any voice in major decisions that affected their lives at work or in the community-at-large.

The first few days of the strike were generally peaceful. Then, on April 5th, Berwind-White took steps to crush the walkout. Notices were sent to the miners ordering them out of the company houses if they didn't report to work. A few of the men drifted back into the mines and coal was again being shipped. It was believed the rest of the miners would soon be back on the job. But thousands of men still defied the company in spite of the fact that they faced eviction from their homes. Tempers were running high and it only needed a spark to set off an explosion among the strikers.

On Easter Monday, April 16th, at three o'clock in the afternoon, some two thousand strikers were gathered in a meadow listening to Genter give a speech. A man believed to be a "spotter" — a company spy — was seen at the edge of the crowd. Several of the miners ran after him and caught him in the center of the town when he fell down exhausted from the chase. A physician, Ellis Davis, rescued the man, but not before the miners had beaten him severely, breaking some of his ribs and ripping off one of his ears.

The Somerset County sheriff, W. C. Begley, with the help of company guards armed with Winchester rifles, arrested ten men for the beating of the spotter and for stoning Davis' house. Dr. Davis, incidentally, was an employee of the company. The arrested men were taken to the Windber jail and locked up. The "guards" were actually the infamous Coal and Iron Police.

In less than a half hour, more than a thousand of the strikers surrounded the jail and, shouting threats and insults, noisily demanded the release of their comrades. In the jail, the company police and deputies, armed with their rifles, stood by the doors and windows. By five PM, just a couple of hours after the trouble started with the chase and beating of the company spy, the strikers began throwing bricks at the jail. One prisoner was turned loose in the hope of appeasing the mob, but the strikers were not satisfied and wanted them all released.

Another bombardment of bricks crashed through the windows of the jail and several guards were knocked off their feet. Warning shots were fired over the heads of the mob. Then a hail of gunfire poured out of the building. No one knows who gave the order to open fire, but three striking miners — 35 year old Steve Popovich, 36 year old Michael Toman, and 28 year old Simon Vorcheck — were instantly killed and a dozen others wounded. The dead immigrants all had wives and children in Europe.

A young boy watching the excitement from the fringe of the crowd, ten-year old Curtis Kester, also was hit by a bullet that lodged in his groin. He ran across the street to a hotel and shouted, "I'm shot!" A night watchman, F.M. Barrett, picked up the boy who looked up into his face and said, "Do you think I'll die?" Barrett, with tears in his eyes, tried to reassure the youth saying, "No, no, you'll be okay." He carried Curtis to the hospital where he died from his wounds two days later.

In addition to Curtis and the miners who were killed and wounded by gunfire, five of the guards suffered serious injuries from flying bricks and broken glass. The mob had now gotten larger and its fury was intensifying. Their wounded were taken to the hospital, but at first they wouldn't allow anyone to touch the dead men. Finally the county coroner arrived and convinced the mob leaders to release the bodies. This brought a lull into the battle and Sheriff Begley quickly sent off a telegram to the State Police barracks in Greensburg, some forty miles away. Captain John Forland, the commander of Troop "A", read the message: *"Unable to cope with riot at Windber. Send troopers at once."*

Forland assigned twenty men to the job. They reached Windber from Greensburg by train at four o'clock on the morning of the 17th, detrained with their horses, and occupied the town. From that moment on, there was no more trouble. The twenty Black Hussars, batons and rifles strapped to their saddles, patrolled the town like an army of occupation. They never had to lift their rifles or batons. The rioting was ended and, within a few weeks, the strike was over. The strikers did not get a union.

There was, however, another side to this story. According to an immigrant newspaper, the *Slovak v Amerike,* when the troopers arrived in Windber, they rode their horses through gatherings of more than two people *"whom they clubbed."* Moreover, the paper said: *"The Pennsylvania State Police's own reports on its occupation of Windber indicate that these troops, exclusively American born and English-speaking, took great delight in forcefully subduing a largely immigrant working-class population of strikers."*

Immigrants began learning about the State Police through the many foreign-language newspapers they read. Southern and eastern European miners popularly referred to the troopers as "Cossacks" because, according to their newspapers, they *"acted like the similarly repressive troops used by the Czar against workers in Russia."*

One drawing in the *Slovak v Amerike* showed five big, burly men sitting on their horses in front of a stable. The caption beneath the picture reads: *"Brave murderers under the Russian law of the State of Pennsylva-*

nia." The drawing, however, does not depict Pennsylvania State Police. The uniforms and horses are not even similar to the ones used by the Black Hussars. Most likely they were Coal Company guards.

Reporters from major newspapers and the wire services, presumably less biased and more factual, presented a somewhat different story about the actions of the troopers. Once the State Police repressed the riot, according to the *Johnstown Tribune,* they simply lined the streets in full gear — guns and batons at their side — and kept the peace without using any force. They were, according to the *Tribune, "treated by the immigrants with great respect."*

The Hussars arrived in Windber on April 17th, restored order immediately, and the next day, on the 18th, the headlines were screaming about the earthquake that wrecked San Francisco. The Berwind-White coal strike and the shooting deaths of three men and a young boy were no longer news in the national press. Even the nearby *Johnstown Tribune* consigned the story to a subservient position to the disaster in San Francisco.

While the nation's attention was focused on California, thousands of immigrants trailed sadly behind the coffins of their dead comrades on the way to the cemetery while the State Police, mounted on their horses, kept a watchful eye out for trouble as the mournful procession passed by. There was no trouble, and the Hussars soon left Windber.

As strikes go, it wasn't the biggest or the bloodiest in which the troopers would become involved. It was significant, however, that within a few weeks after taking to the field for the first time, the Pennsylvania State Police quickly and convincingly crushed riots in both the hard and soft coal regions of the State. This action at the outset of its existence gained the Force an immediate national notoriety as a group of men who would not be intimidated nor could they be disobeyed. Their reputation for unrelenting efficiency grew and stayed with them for decades. The performance of the troopers during their first month in the field also resulted in the labels pinned on them by immigrants — "Black Hussars" and "Cossacks."

14.

WILHELM

Cecil M. Wilhelm was born in Reading, Pennsylvania on October 21, 1881. He was an excellent horseman and was a varsity football player at the Pennsylvania Military College. One of his teammates, Cecil B. DeMille, went on to become a Hollywood founder and its' most famous director and producer.

Wilhelm was West Point bound when the Spanish-American war broke out. As a member of the Pennsylvania National Guard, he was called into active service and saw action in the war's Puerto Rican campaign. He remained in military service until 1905 when he joined the newly formed Pennsylvania State Police and was given the rank of Sergeant at Troop B in Wilkes-Barre. After meritorious service and passing numerous tests, he became a Captain of the State Police in 1911.

Wilhelm, at the urging of Superintendent Groome, accepted a Captaincy in the U.S. Army Signal Corps in 1917 and saw service in World War I in Europe where he rose to the rank of Major. He remained in the Army until April of 1919 when he returned to his old post with the State Police.

Wilhelm was appointed Superintendent of the Pennsylvania State Police in 1943 at the age of 61. He held this post for twelve years and it was his desire to retire in the summer of 1955 when he would have fifty years of service on the Force. In January of 1955, George M. Leader took the oath of office to become only the second Democratic Party Governor since the turn of the century. Wilhelm was forced to resign his post just short of fifty years with the State Police. Governor Leader was not an unkind person, but he was a politician and politics had by now become a part of the State Police. Wilhelm had stepped on the wrong toes and an illustrious career came to an end. He was the last of the original Black Hussars.

105

THE BLACK HUSSARS

Hughestown is a coal mining community in Luzerne County, not too far from Pittston in Eastern Pennsylvania. Hughestown possessed, as Katherine Mayo put it in her inimitable style: *"...its share of decent, orderly, English-speaking miner folk, and it also possessed a gang of Italian banditti more brazen and bloody here than they had dreamed of being in their own Sicilian hills."*

Among themselves, the immigrants seemed to have a propensity for getting into rambling altercations that often led to fist fights which in turn led to knife fights. The "decent, English-speaking miner folk" would look upon this brawling and bloodshed taking place in "Little Italy" with stoic indifference: *"Small harm, for they only kill each other."*

In the spring of 1906, a contagious disease broke out in the Italian community and, as was the custom up until World War II, the town policeman, Jacob Schmaltz, posted the houses with quarantine signs. The tenants promptly tore down the signs and were just as promptly arrested and fined. Schmaltz became their enemy.

In the meantime, the "banditti" in "Little Italy" began to prowl the countryside outside of their community and threatened anyone who got in their way. Schmaltz was practically helpless. The townspeople were no longer indifferent to the antics in the Italian community.

On a warm summer evening a couple of months after the posting and fines, three teenaged Italian immigrants grabbed sixteen year old Helen McAllister as she was walking along a dusty road just on the outskirts of the town. Scared out of her wits, the attractive young girl screamed for help as she furiously fought with her attackers. Officer Schmaltz heard her cries and rushed to aid the girl. Thomas Loftus, a 22 year old miner on his way home from work, was nearby when the girl's screams pierced the air. In less than a minute, he was at the side of the town policeman throwing punches at the three young men. The trio of thugs was run off, but not before they somehow found out the name of Loftus and subsequently learned where he lived.

A week later, while Tom and his father Michael were still at work, Mrs. Loftus answered a knock on her door. She was greeted by a darkly handsome, young Italian who coolly informed her that her son would never reach home alive as he and his friends intended to kill him and then take care of the rest of the family at their leisure. The frightened woman slammed the door in the face of the brazen youth and then bolted it. Within minutes, the house was bombarded with stones by a mob of immigrants.

Mrs. Loftus gathered her two daughters and slipped out the back door of her home. Running unseen into some woods at the back of the house, the mother and daughters managed to make their way into the town where they told officer Schmaltz about the mob. Realizing he would be unable to control the situation by himself, Schmaltz put in a call to B Troop barracks of the State Police in Wyoming, just on the other side of the river from Wilkes-Barre and about seven miles south of Hughestown. Privates John S. Garland, Homer Adelson, and Matthew Butler were dispatched to the scene of the trouble. It took them, on horseback, about thirty minutes of fast riding to get to Hughestown.

When the three troopers arrived, they found the Loftus house still surrounded by a gang of ruffians. With batons drawn and using their horses, the Black Hussars immediately began to disperse the mob. As they were herding them away, a shot rang out from the side of the road. Garland was dropped from the saddle with a bullet through his lung. The other two troopers turned toward the firing. As soon as Adelson and Butler drew their weapons, Adelson was shot and went down with a bullet in his side. Alone, Butler, firing his pistol, charged his horse into the gang, which broke and fled into the Italian quarter of town. With his two partners on the ground bleeding from bullet wounds, Butler asked an onlooker to get a doctor and to call the State Police barracks for assistance. "Tell them what has happened here," he said.

The wounded troopers were carried into the Loftus home and given what aid gathering neighbors could render until a doctor could get to the injured men. Butler, meanwhile, sat his horse, guarded the house and waited for help to arrive from troop headquarters.

Cutting through fields and farmlands, Sgt. Cecil Wilhelm and ten troopers made it to Hughestown in just over an hour from the time Garland

and Adelson were gunned down. Wasting no time, Wilhelm assessed the situation and then immediately led the Black Hussars into the Italian community where members of the mob had fled and barricaded themselves in various houses. Following Sgt. Wilhelm, the black clad police kicked down the doors of the homes and, with batons swinging, the troopers dragged men out of cellars, from attics, pulled them from under beds and ransacked the houses. Those mob members who were wounded, (many of them), were carried to the hospital. The rest were hauled off to jail.

A terrified Mrs. Loftus returned home with her daughters and was calmed by Sgt. Wilhelm with assurance that a guard would be placed on her house that night. He also set a guard over the Italian section of town where the troopers stayed for several days until peace was assured. Privates Adelson and Garland eventually recovered from their wounds and returned to duty.

Just a month earlier Captain Loftus had sent troopers to put down rioting at the Fernwood colliery at a place called "Boston Patch" near Wilkes-Barre. Using the same tactics as they used in Hughestown, the Black Hussars had broken down doors to confiscate weapons. The troopers in the Boston Patch fray were then taken into court by the United Mine Workers Union for trespassing, but they were quickly acquitted.

There were no charges leveled against them at Hughestown. Instead, the press was full of praise for the troopers. The day after the battle, the *Pittston Gazette* printed an editorial applauding the Black Hussars: *"...it is the most serious local action the Troop has yet encountered and they bore themselves in such soldierly fashion as to deserve praise on all sides ... It will be surprising if there is not a great falling off in the demand for the repeal of the Constabulary Act by the next Legislature."*

Well, not *all* the press was full of praise. On the other side of the state, the *Johnstown Democrat* said the Hughestown affair had been merely a little innocent horseplay. *"It was a holiday, and the Italians were celebrating in their peculiar noisy and demonstrative way. Pennypacker's Cossacks rushed in and turned harmless merrymaking into a scene of blood."* The newspaper asked if Pennsylvania was really *"prepared to turn over civil authority to a band of mercenaries"* for the pleasure of a Governor who *"has at his command roving bodies of armed men acting under his orders."*

Interestingly, the *Democrat* was a newspaper strongly supportive of the union movement and every cause put forward by the immigrants, but it was extremely critical of the action taken by the State Police to protect the Loftus family, although Thomas Loftus and all his male relatives were members of the United Mine Workers of America, the biggest union in the State.

15.

THE PHILADELPHIA CAR STRIKE

At first it was just an awed whisper among a few people; *"The Hussars."* Within minutes the whisper became louder and spread like a prairie fire up and down Broad Street. *"The Black Hussars! The Black Hussars are coming!"* It was a gray, bitter cold day and the wind off the Delaware River only added to the chill felt by the onlookers as they awaited the arrival of the Pennsylvania State Police.

February 19, 1910.   Six thousand employees of the Philadelphia Rapid Transit System went out on strike.   The walkout quickly developed into riot conditions.   Gangs of roughs, known as "hooligan boys," and described as "not strikers, but strike sympathizers," joined with the union men in the labor dispute.   Between the six thousand strikers and the "hooligan boys," Philadelphia's three thousand city policemen were unable to control the situation.

A militia organization named the State Fencibles was called upon to help the city police.   These were young society men whose most notable accomplishment seemed to be the ability to come up with the price of fancy uniforms. The mob roaming the streets at first laughed at them and amused itself by cutting off the gold buttons on the front of the Fencibles uniforms. Then the hooligan boys hung pretzels on the bayonets of the guns carried by the Fencibles and, laughing all the time, the young toughs took away their rifles.   Soon, however, the humor darkened, the mood of the hooligans grew ugly, and the mob began to beat the society men and throw them through windows.   The Fencibles were finally rescued by the police and retreated to their armory to lick their wounds.

The strike turned even more violent and soon resulted in widespread destruction of property. On February 21st, a pitched battle was fought at the Baldwin Locomotive Works, just four blocks from the City Hall courtyard. It was touched off during the noon lunch hour when employees at Baldwin attacked a trolley car. The motorman was knocked out with a rock and the car was destroyed.

Hundreds of police reserves were deployed from City Hall and moved down Broad Street in an effort to break up the rioters. Several thousand strikers and their allies gathered around the Baldwin plant and hurled rocks at the police. Then, from the windows of the plant, a rain of iron missiles, bolts, nuts and iron bars, poured down on the attacking men in blue. Scores of policemen were knocked off their feet and injured. The police replied with gunfire aimed through the windows of the plant. From behind a brick wall, strike sympathizers sent another hail of missiles while men on the upper floors and roof of the plant exposed themselves to the gunfire and taunted the police about their marksmanship.

The superintendent at the Baldwin Works went among the men and ordered them back to work. Asserting his authority, a brief lull descended over the bloody scene, but the men were in too ugly a mood to stay calm. Armed with iron bars, they left the plant and formed a mob outside the Works. At that moment, several trolley cars came down the street and tried to run the blockade. The first attack on the cars was a shower of stones from the front ranks of the rioters. Then the men with iron bars charged, pushed back the police and swarmed over the trolleys. The howl of the mob could be heard for blocks intermingled with gunshots and screams as skulls were cracked and bullets found a human mark. Policemen riding guard on the trolleys were thrown bodily into the crowd.

More police reserves arrived and the two sides battled furiously; the mob with their iron bars and the police firing their guns and striking savagely with their billy clubs. The street war raged on; back and forth, clubbing and cursing, each side refusing to give ground. Then, after what seemed like hours but was really less than a half hour, the strikers got their own reinforcements as more men poured out of the Baldwin plant and the over-whelming outnumbered police retreated to City Hall.

When the smoke finally cleared from the battle, five persons were dead or dying from injuries, scores were seriously injured, seven hundred trolley cars were wrecked, five thousand car windows were smashed, dynamite was used to destroy some of the cars, and more than one thousand men had been arrested.

The New York World said of the battle: *"The entire police reserves were driven in rout to the stockade within the City Hall courtyard. The city police then admitted that they could no longer cope with the situation."*

The Director of Public Safety and the Superintendent of City Police called on Governor Edwin Stuart to turn out the National Guard. Stuart said that would be too costly and, besides, it wasn't necessary. He would send in the State Police. "When the mob has eaten up the State Police," he said, "then I will give you the Guard."

The proposal was criticized and widely jeered as folly. How, the city leaders asked, could fewer than two hundred strangers handle a huge mob that had defied, worn out, and beaten more than three thousand heavily reinforced trained officers on their own turf? But with the howls of the mob ringing through City Hall, the Mayor had no choice and could wait no longer.

On February 22nd, the *Philadelphia Ledger* ran a special edition telling of the Governor's offer and the Mayor's acceptance. *"The State Mounted Police from the coal regions,"* ran the story, *"hated and dreaded and known as the Black Hussars, will be coming to Philadelphia to put down the rioting. They fire to kill and carry automatic guns."*

John J. Murphy, president of the Central Labor Union, was furious and declared "...the instant the Black Hussars make an appearance on the city's streets I will call out 100,000 men and inaugurate the bitterest strike that any city in the country has ever experienced."

By afternoon of that same day, the order went out to the State Police barracks in the four corners of the state. Another order went out from the barracks to the substations calling in the men. Some of them, in substations as far as thirty miles away, had to travel that distance on horseback before they could join their Troops. At six o'clock on the night of February 23rd, the men of "A" Troop, at Greensburg in the western part of the state, were boarding a train with their horses. At 6:30 PM, "B" Troop at Wilkes-

Barre in the eastern part of the state, was marching through the streets to the railway station while townspeople cheered like Englishmen sending Kitchener's troops off to rescue Gordon at Khartoum. By five o'clock the following morning, all four Troops rendezvoused west of Philadelphia where the men and horses gathered onto one train for their entrance into the city.

The Black Hussars arrived in Philadelphia early in the morning of Thursday, February 24th, 1910. Almost all the troopers in the State Police Force, one hundred and seventy eight men, led their horses off the train at the Broad Street station. The entire Force was there except for a few men left behind to guard the barracks and to look after raw recruits.

On the other side of the state, the newspapers were having a field day. On that same Thursday evening, the three column headlines and sub-heads of the *Johnstown Tribune* blared:

BLACK HORSE CAVALRY TO SUBDUE STRIKE

Arrival of the State Constabulary, Mounted and Displaying Automatic Firearms, Increases Feeling of Tension

State Troopers Prepared to Ride Down Crowds Without Mercy on First Show of Disorder

Population of Disturbed Districts is Visibly Excited Over Prospect of Encounter with Well-Known Mob Fighters, in Spite of Small Number of Constabulary as Compared with City Police

The night before the Troopers arrived in town, a meeting of Philadelphia police officials and city leaders was held at City Hall. The Director of Public Safety, William Stuart, and his police captains came up with a plan to divide the State Police squadron into groups of eight to ten men and assign them to each ward of the city.

Afterward, Stuart sent for John C. Groome, the Superintendent of the State Police. Stuart outlined the plan for using the troopers in small detachments to augment the city police. The Public Safety Director and his captains were astonished by Groome's answer. As General "Black Jack" Pershing would do seven years in the future, rejecting the French and English demand to use American troops to fill the gaps in their own depleted armies, Groome absolutely refused to go along with Stuart's plan. Later, Groome explained his refusal and his reasoning: *"I realized the danger that would lie in my men's working with city police, under divided authority and with no one really responsible for any mistakes that might occur. When they asked me what I would do to help contain the rioting, I said that if they would give me a certain section of the city...they could take all their men off the streets at eight o'clock the next morning, and I would be responsible for the maintenance of law and order in my section. I knew exactly what part of the city they would give me, Kensington, where they had the most trouble — and they did."*

Kensington was Philadelphia's manufacturing center and the sector of the city where, as Groome knew, all the violence was taking place. It was an area of dirty streets and verminous yards — even in bright sunlight the rows of neglected houses, nestled in among the factories, were mean and dejected, their grimy windows looking out in blank hostility on the world. The city police, Stuart said, needed a rest. Groome smiled and told Stuart that his men would be willing to patrol that region of the city and do what they could to restore order. When the meeting was over, Groome grabbed a few hours sleep and then went to the train station to await his men.

Witnesses to the arrival of the State Police force into that riot-torn section of the City of Brotherly Love said it was a majestic sight of contained power. Groome himself led the long line of horsemen that advanced at a walk in a column of twos. His deputy, Captain George Lumb, rode by his side. The troopers looked straight ahead without even a hint of nervous tension. Veterans of numerous campaigns and battles in China, the Philippines, Puerto Rico and Cuba, the Hussars were lean and stern, sitting their horses like centaurs. Black horses. Black, somber uniforms. Black helmets whose visors shaded eyes that looked neither to the right nor left. Big, black holsters, hanging heavy from the full cartridge belts and long riot sticks hanging from the saddle horns. They had not brought their carbines because, as Groome put it, *"We don't need them here."*

OFF TO PHILADELPHIA

State troopers from the Wyoming barracks on their way to the railroad station in 1910. The men shown here joined up with troopers from other parts of the state to quell rioting in Philadelphia.

Slashes of pink streaked the sky as the sun slowly rose to light up the East Coast. The wind whipped coldly against the striking workers and their allies as they hunched forward against the aggression of nature. The full measure of winter was almost gone, but winds and cold would sweep through the city for another month. The invisible onslaught of nature, however, was not what worried the strikers, but rather the very visible Black Cavalry heading into the city.

As the troopers moved toward the streets of Kensington, a whisper moved before them like wind in the trees. *"The Black Hussars! They're coming!"* An observer wrote, *"The streets emptied. The troopers might have been mounted genie, so quickly was their quieting presence felt."*

THE BLACK HUSSARS

Without a word spoken or a command voiced, the crowd that had gathered to curse or stone the "Black Hussars" disappeared into alleys and houses as though they were swallowed up. Silently, with only the clopping of the horses' hooves, the mounted column moved through the streets while from nearby houses a shutter or curtain moved as hidden eyes peered out at the troopers, and a few women, children and sullen men, arms crossed, glared at the Hussars from the sidewalks.

As the squadron moved farther into the heart of the district, a strike sympathizer hurled a steel bolt from the window of a factory hitting a trooper in the back. The assailant instantly ducked out of sight, but not quickly enough to escape the eye of the officer next to the man hit by the missile. The column came to a halt as a trooper vaulted from his saddle and swiftly moved into the factory. Striding alone through its crowded halls and up several flights of stairs, he reached the floor from which the bolt was thrown. With one glance at the mass of glowering men packed in the room, he singled out the assailant. Ignoring the rest of the men as though they didn't exist, he grabbed the bolt thrower by the back of the neck and propelled him past his friends, down the stairs, out of the building, and into custody. Just the day before, the throwing of that bolt would have set off a riot and blood-shed. Now, not a finger was raised, not a voice was heard to resist the arrest.

Captain Groome decided to quarter the men and their horses in the trolley car barn at Eighth and Dauphin streets in the heart of the Kensington district. Hitching posts were driven for the horses, the officers found space to sleep in the company office, and the troopers were given shakedowns of straw on the floor for their rest.

A short time after their arrival at the car barn, the squadron was divided into small groups and deployed over the entire riot-torn district. The area was so great compared to the size of the Force and the vigilance required, that each trooper was compelled to remain on duty eighteen hours a day. A number of arrests were made the first day on patrol, but then quiet set in and was almost unbroken for the remainder of the State Police stay in Philadelphia.

Most men would have been daunted by the situation the troopers found upon their arrival in Philadelphia. They had very little rest and were vastly outnumbered by a hostile force of tough workers, but the Black Hussars welcomed the challenge. They simply got up even earlier and patrolled longer into the darkness. When fatigue laid a hand on them, they never showed it. If obstacles fell across their path, they leapt nimbly over them. If anything even began to depress their spirits, they invoked the memory of fallen comrades and the indomitable resolve of their Superintendent and carried on with restored vigor. It was impossible to oppose the Black Hussars. They were invincible.

From the second day that the State Police arrived in the city, the trolley cars ran throughout the district in perfect safety. One rumor made the rounds and found its way into the newspapers that the troopers once or twice fired volleys at the mob. The story, however, was completely without foundation. The Force, during its entire tour of duty, fired not a single shot.

On February 25, the day after the Hussars' arrival, the Philadelphia *North American* ran a story that said in part: *"Their first appearance here on serious business awakened for them the respect and admiration of the whole town ...No sooner had they trotted into position than they became the observed of all the observers... They sat their saddles with a quite force that stirred a glint of admiration in almost every eye that took them in ...They were quiet and steady to talk to, and they did not do any boasting ...These men are noted for the accuracy and dispatch with which they do business. They are cool, but when they get started they move like a shot. They have come to camp here in the interest of law and order; and if you doubt their ability to swing things as they want them to be swung, just journey up to the district and look one of them in the eye. You won't make any impolite remarks to him."*

The next day the *North American* carried a follow-up story: *"...the black-coated police seem to have made a very favorable impression. Few people have harsh words for them and in the few arrests they have been forced to make they have carried themselves coolly and sensibly."*

THE BLACK HUSSARS

The exploits of the Pennsylvania State Police, less than five years after its formation, weren't confined to Philadelphia or even to Pennsylvania. Stories were being written about the Black Hussars in places as far away as Minnesota, and the editorial writers of newspapers across the land were asking why state police forces were not being formed in their own states.

The *New York Sun* of February 26, 1910 did a side bar to their coverage of the Philadelphia strike noting that: *"...Captain Jack Groome's cavalrymen ... came here expecting real trouble ... they met practically no resistance.*

"Prompt and summary action by these men, backed up by their reputation ... created a wholesome respect for their prowess. They have a reputation of getting the man they go after. They showed several times this afternoon how they do it.

"A young man in Germantown Avenue was foolish enough to shout bad names at one of the troopers. He was warned once to keep his mouth shut, but, encouraged by the applause of the crowd, he finally uttered a really nasty remark and the trooper leaped from his horse, ripped through the crowd and yanked the youth from a cigar store where he had taken refuge. The crowd murmured threateningly, but nobody lifted a hand to rescue the young man in the grasp of the Black Hussar. Meanwhile, the trooper's horse stood rigidly where he had been left, his bridle rein hanging over his neck. The trooper turned his prisoner over to a city cop and the young man was dumped into a patrol wagon. Then the trooper remounted his horse and slowly continued his patrol of the avenue."

All the papers were now filled with picturesque stories of the buoyant adventures of the "Black Hussars." Meantime, the newspapers back in the home districts of the troopers were asking with proprietary jealousy whether Philadelphia grasped the value of the sacrifice those small towns were making and, if you please, they would like to have their State Police back to patrol the countryside they left in order to put down the troubles in the City of Brotherly Love.

By March 1st, the "insurrection" was all but over and the *Philadel-*

phia Ledger editorialized: *"It is not their horsemanship, not their revolvers or their riot sticks, that makes this handful of men a terror to riotous law-breakers ... and an insurance of safety to peaceful citizens. They represent no class or condition, no prejudice or interest, nothing but the sovereign majesty of the law. Hostility to them is hostility to the people whose authority they represent We need at all times, and especially in times of disturbance, to keep this one thought uppermost in our minds, that the source of all authority, the foundation of our liberty, the assurance of our safety, is not in the utterances of any men, be they wise or foolish, but in the government of law, which the people have established, and which every one of us owes his best service to maintain. Men, parties, and factions come and go; there remains for our unshaken allegiance the name and authority of the Commonwealth of Pennsylvania."*

All over the nation the leaders of the press continued to talk about the actions of the Pennsylvania State Police and how they ended the riots that had erupted in Philadelphia. Almost all the newspapers agreed that it was a magnificent display of controlled force and coolness coupled with dignity and fairness. The one thing nobody seemed to be able to get right was the proper name for this State Police Force. On March 18, 1910, the New York *Evening Post* calling them the Constabulary, editorially summarized what most of the nation's press was thinking:

"The Philadelphia street railway strike ought not to slip from the public mind without attention being called again to one highly important phase of the battle between order and disorder in the city streets. We refer to the invaluable service of the Pennsylvania State Constabulary. After the expected failure of the city's police to control the lawless strikers, and the pitiful incapacity of a battalion of militia to patrol one street, the Constabulary was sent for ... The arrival of only one hundred and eighty of the Constabulary changed the entire situation; thereafter disorder practically ceased. What several thousand city policemen failed to accomplish, the Constabulary did in a twinkling, and in a way to compel the enthusiastic admiration of all beholders. And there is a reason for the difference. The Constabulary is a business organization. Although employed by the State,

119

it knows no politics in its make-up, or in the execution of its orders. It is an object lesson to the entire country, because it proves that it is not necessary that we should have, as a nation, the worst police in the world, and because it suggests, to all who stop to think, one reason why Europe, with its constabulary, is so vastly more law-abiding than the United States."...

"When the bill creating this force was passed in Harrisburg in 1905, we commented upon its purport as one of the most important developments in American government of recent years. Everything we hoped of it has been realized and more besides ... It is the cheapest investment that the State has ever made, and its record answers every excuse, wherever made, that other States cannot do likewise because of lack of funds. If the situation is but studied, it will soon be found that no State can afford to do without a similar body ... New York and every other state should have them."

It would take another half dozen years before New York had its own state police force. In the meantime, while the Pennsylvania State Police quickly, and in most cases without bloodshed, restored order in labor disputes, other states were not quite so fortunate.

In the fall of 1913, for example, 9,000 miners went on strike in the coal fields of southern Colorado. They were looking to improve their working conditions and gain recognition of their union, the UMW. Expecting to be evicted from their company-owned houses, they set up tent cities for their families near the company towns. The mine owners promptly recruited armed men, much like the old Coal and Iron Police of Pennsylvania.

Sporadic harassment of the miners by the armed guards took place for the next several months. On April 20, 1914, two hundred armed company guards suddenly attacked the main tent city near Ludlow. They fired indiscriminately into the tents for hours, then soaked them with kerosene and set them ablaze. When the shooting finally stopped, at least 21 persons were dead and 100 wounded. In spite of the slaughter, the strike continued for another eight months, but the mine operators eventually won.

Prior to the formation of the Pennsylvania State Police, just as in

Colorado, death, destruction and repression of the miners was common in the coal fields of the Keystone State. But after the Black Hussars took to the field, working men learned that the State Police Force was their only defense against unlawful aggressions by the mine operators. Moreover, the miner, steel worker, and the working man in general, saw the State Police as his own police, his own best protector. Houses saved from burning, pay-envelopes saved from highway robbers, stolen goods recovered and returned, lost children traced and found, working girls rescued from assailants, gangs broken up and removed, and communities made safe thanks to the Black Hussars.

But the admiration many of the working families and union members had for the troopers did not always carry over to the labor leaders. For years they continued their efforts to first, have the Force disbanded and, when those efforts failed, they tried to dilute its authority by making it more susceptible to political influence. Over time — by the middle of the century — the political efforts bore fruit among the ever-growing hierarchy of the Force. But even to this day, a vast majority of troopers in the field remain true to the principles and canons laid down by Superintendent Groome. As for the first several decades of their existence, the members of the Force, from top to bottom, looked upon politics as an anathema.

TEDDY ROOSEVELT PRAISES POLICE

" ...the State Police of Pennsylvania ... has furnished a model which is to be studied everywhere; and we Americans ought to be pleased that it is no longer necessary for us to study the excellent Canadian Northwestern Police, or the excellent Argentine Police, when we desire to find how the elementary needs of our States can best be served in securing law, order, and justice.

The Pennsylvania State Police is a model of efficiency, a model of honesty, a model of absolute freedom from political contamination ... there is no other body so emphatically efficient for modern needs as the Pennsylvania State Police. I have seen them at work. I feel so strongly about them that the mere fact that a man is honorably discharged from this Force would make me at once, and without hesitation, employ him for any purpose needing courage, prowess, good judgment, loyalty, and entire trustworthiness. The men are capital riders, good shots, and as sound and strong in body and mind as in character.

... The sooner all our other States adopt similar systems, the better it will be for the cause of law and order, and for the upright administration of the laws in the interests of justice throughout the Union."

Theodore Roosevelt November 10, 1916

TEDDY VISITS HUSSARS

The State troopers at Troop B barracks in Wyoming, PA wear "Rough Rider" hats in honor of former President Theodore Roosevelt who visited with the men in 1910. Many of the troopers served in the Spanish-American War.

THE BLACK HUSSARS

PART IV
THE BLACK HAND

THE BLACK HUSSARS

..from the microfiche ...

AMERICANS AT COURT MAKE GERMANY HOWL WITH RAGE

Press of the Fatherland Roars with Anger when Kaiser Shows Imperial Favor to Mere Commoners From Across the Atlantic

Berlin   Jan. 21, 1910 – "Berlin's social leaders are in revolt today over the presentation to the Kaiser and Kaiserin at last night's court recognition of 28 Americans, mostly women, but few of whom, according to German court etiquette, were entitled to participation in such an exclusive function.... Letting down the bars to Americans of various ranks has raised a storm of protest ... such consideration was never before shown to the people of any foreign country ... the Germans had to admit, however, that the dresses and jewels worn by the Americans easily outshone the Germans' raiment."

"And the ladies of the harem
Knew exactly how to wear 'em
In Oriental Baghdad long ago."

... from the classifieds...

FOR SALE: Ten-room house. Lot 95 X 100 feet. City water, electric light. House in excellent shape, 100 feet from trolley line. Price: $5,000 - half down, rest on time.   Phone H.K. Taylor at 614.

GIRLS WANTED: to work on shirts. Good steady workers can earn from $4.50 to $8 a week. This is nice, clean, and easy work, and we will guarantee steady work throughout the year. Apply to the Johnstown Shirt Factory.

A BOWL OF POST TOASTIES

A pleasure and comfort for old and young, at any meal,

at any time, anywhere! Let a bowlful in front of you tell

its own delightful story!   Sold by grocers.

5 cents for a large package!

Postum Cereal Co., Battlecreek, Mich.

GIRLS ARE ROASTED TO DEATH OR
KILLED JUMPING FROM WINDOWS

**Over Score May Be Dead in Burning of Philadelphia
Shirt Factory Building**

THE PLACE WAS A FIRE TRAP
**Men Driven From Work of Rescue Because
They Could Not Stand the Awful Sight**

ALL ESCAPE CUT OFF BY FALLING WALLS

"It takes nerve to live in this world"
Last Words of George Smith Hanged with his Brother
By Mob in Kansas

128

16.

During the first ten years of the Pennsylvania State Police, the Troopers made nearly 28,000 arrests. None of those people taken into custody were charged with striking against their employers, nor do the words "labor dispute" appear in the records of the State Police. There were, however, about two thousand people out of the 28,000 arrested, who were charged with unlawful assembly, trespassing, dynamiting, threats, resisting arrest, rioting, surety of the peace, and interfering with an officer. It might be assumed that many of those people, perhaps most of them, were indeed involved in labor strikes. Still, that would leave some 26,000 persons who were arrested by the State Police for other crimes ranging from murder to violation of the Sabbath laws - such as drinking alcohol on Sunday.

Breaking the Sabbath laws, as well as being a pauper, were crimes and not misdemeanors. Of those 295 people arrested for violating the Sabbath laws, 294 were convicted. Misdemeanor was a category all by itself. During those ten years, two people were arrested and convicted for "trover," a common-law action to recover damages for property illegally withheld or wrongfully converted to use by another.

In any case, the two hundred or so Black Hussars patrolling thousands of miles of Pennsylvania countryside, small towns and villages, were evidently kept pretty busy fighting crime in general. This, in addition to putting down riots and upholding law and order during labor disputes that turned ugly. With the exception of the McKees Rocks "Massacre," where two troopers were killed during a bitter strike against the Pressed Steel Car Company, the other eight troopers killed during this period died while performing duties unconnected with strikes or riots.

Despite dire warnings from legislators aligned with the unions and a few labor-oriented newspapers that complained the State Police Force was only another name for the infamous Coal and Iron Police, the Force was, in fact, created to uphold the law in rural areas of the Commonwealth. True, in the first decade of their existence, the Black Hussars spent a lot of time successfully putting the lid on mob violence, usually related to a labor strike, but crime of every imaginable description came under their jurisdiction and therefore took up most of their time.

Of all the crimes and criminals the State Police investigated, one group of outlaws stood out from the rest. They committed every serious crime on the books including extortion, kidnapping, attempted murder, assault and battery, murder, and a host of other heinous acts. This group, the Black Hand Society, developed an effective, organized, inter-state operation and is widely believed to be the forerunner to the "Mafia" in the United States. The Black Hand, a secret society of extortionists, was operating some years before the State Police came into existence and its activities were by no means confined to Pennsylvania. The work of the Black Hussars, between 1907 and 1916, practically wiped out the influence of these outlaws in the rural and smaller cities of the State, but not without a heavy price to the troopers. The first two Hussars to be killed fell to bullets from the guns of Blank Hand members.

HUSSARS MAKE THE MOVIES

"I have constructed a little instrument," Thomas Edison wrote in 1893, *"which I call a Kinetoscope, with a nickel and a slot attachment. Some 25 have been made, but I am very doubtful if there is any commercial future in it."*

It was the beginning of the motion picture industry. That year the "little instrument," forerunner of the projector, presented the first film. It featured a man sneezing. Feature films soon followed. (Of these, D.W. Griffith's 1915 production, *The Birth of a Nation*, was the boldest, the most controversial, and the most successful.)

By 1910, ten thousand American movie houses had weekly audiences of ten million people. Mary Pickford was America's Sweetheart and earning one million dollars a year. It seemed like everyone in the nation was going to the movies. In those days, in addition to the feature film, theaters would show what they called "short subjects", a version of today's documentary.

The Black Hussars arrested scores of kidnappers prior to the advent of the Lindbergh Law. This photo, however, looks as though it came from the movie made about the State Police.

At this time, the Pennsylvania State Police had attracted favorable notice throughout the country and a motion picture studio wanted to do a short subject on the Black Hussars. Studio officials sent a film crew to the Troop A headquarters at Greensburg. Captain Lynn Adams, head of the Troop, with permission from Harrisburg, agreed to cooperate with the filmmakers in their production about the Pennsylvania State Police that was shown in theaters throughout the country.

The plot of the story was not very complicated. The script centered on a kidnapped child who was returned safely to her parents thanks to the efforts of the Black Hussars. It wrapped up with the Troopers successfully prosecuting the case.

An interesting sidebar to the story involves the mascot of the Troopers - a female beagle. The dog was introduced to members of the film crew who, to their surprise and delight, found out that the beagle, Troop A's sweetheart, answered to the name "Mary Pickford".

... from the microfiche...

LUSITANIA BLOWN UP BY GERMANS

The torpedo struck the starboard bow and apparently blew up a boiler. The giant English luxury ship at once began to heel and sink. In the quarter hour before it went under, there was a frantic rush to the lifeboats. Some 700 got away. But 1,198 passengers and crewmen perished; 128 of them Americans. *New York Times May 1915*

(Germany justified the sinking on the grounds the ship carried munitions for England and that passengers were warned in New York newspaper "ADVERTISEMENTS" not to sail on the vessel.)

Woodrow Wilson Re-elected President
His Followers Boast, "He kept us out of war!"

THOUSANDS OF MEN SEEK JOBS IN
FORD MOTOR FACTORY
No Employee to Receive Less Than Five Dollars a Day

...by 1914 Henry Ford was worrying about unfair distribution of profits and in a raucous meeting he proposed raising the daily minimum wages for his workers to three dollars a day, then $3.50, and finally $4.75 and his angry partner James Couzens snapped *"I dare you to make it five dollars"* and Ford did, astounding the nation...

17.

FIRST TO DIE

The Force had gotten off to an excellent start. From March of 1906, when they first went into the field with their new uniforms and equipment, until the end of summer, the Black Hussars rolled up an enviable record of enforcing the State laws including the control of mobs and rioters, usually during labor disputes. March, April, May, June, July, and August — one "triumph" after another. Then, on September 2, 1906, tragedy struck the freshmen troopers before their first year in the field was half over.

Sergeant Joseph Logan of Troop D at Punxsutawney tried to arrest two "Black Hand Society" gangsters in the small mining community of Florence in Jefferson County. The men had been charged with murder and when Logan attempted to take them into custody, the gangsters opened fire on him and then fled into a house where four other members of the "Society" were holed up. Logan called his barracks and requested assistance. Five troopers were sent to aid him and, when they approached the house and demanded to be let in, the answer they got was a volley of gunfire. Three of the six troopers went down in the hail of bullets. Thirty-one years old Private John Henry was instantly killed before gaining entry to the house. Privates Homer Chambers of Rochester, Pennsylvania and William Mullin of Harrisburg, were wounded.

Chambers, although hurting badly from gunshot wounds in the face as well as the arm and sides, went back to get Henry's body in spite of a salvo from the house which resulted in still more wounds to Chambers. (It was believed that Chambers would die, but he survived and was later praised by Groome for his bravery) The three remaining troopers again tried to rush the house. Thirty-four years old Private Francis Zehringer got inside the home before being fatally gunned down. The other two troopers were driven back to cover where they exchanged periodic gunfire with the fugitives while awaiting more help from Troop D headquarters and making sure that

THE ULTIMATE SACRIFICE

HENRY   **ZEHRINGER**
Privates John Henry and Francis Zehringer shot down in September, 1906, were the first two
troopers killed in action. Henry and Zehringer, along with other troopers, were attacking a
stronghold of the Black Hand Society in a mining community near Punxsatawney, PA.

none of the wanted men escaped.

Reinforcements arrived just as nightfall and heavy rain descended on the scene. Captain Joseph Robinson waited until daybreak and, when the men inside continued to fire on the troopers and refused to surrender, Robertson decided to dynamite the house. Under the protection of intense fire by the troopers, Sgt. George Lumb (who would later become Groome's assistant and then the second Superintendent of the Force) and Sgt. William Marsh dashed to the house and retrieved the body of Zehringer. At the same time, another detail of troopers planted dynamite by the house. Both details came under heavy fire from within the house as they made their way back to cover and joined the rest of the troop. After one final warning that was ignored, the dynamite was detonated and the fugitive bastion collapsed and burned killing its occupants. The State was saved the cost of trying and hanging the accused fugitive murderers.

(An investigation and trial was later held and the State Police were exonerated of any wrongdoing, but the owner of the house was reimbursed

134

$3500 for the destruction of his property.)

In the aftermath of the battle, a wagon escorted by troopers bore the bodies of Henry and Zehringer back to the barracks in Punxsutawney where the two fallen Black Hussars laid in state until the following day. From there the bodies of the two slain troopers would be sent to their hometowns for burial. The *Punxsutawney Weekly Spirit* described the funeral procession the next day as one that: *"...will not soon be forgotten by the thousands from Punxsutawney and neighboring towns who witnessed it. Captain Robinson and Lt. Egle rode at the head of the procession with ministers and prominent residents of the city following in carriages. Two hearses carried the bodies of the slain troopers and were followed by four troopers on each side of the hearses, one in each group leading the horses that Zehringer and Henry had ridden, the saddles of which were draped in black. The other troopers, 25 in number, followed on horseback. With bowed heads, the great throng watched the procession proceed to the East End depot, from where the bodies were sent to their respective homes over the Pennsylvania Railroad.*

There are many differences of opinion regarding the manner of conducting the attack on the house which resulted in the slaughter, but all who watched agreed that the courage and loyalty of the State Policemen was beyond criticism."

Private Henry had been born in New York City and, before joining the Pennsylvania State Police, served in the U.S. Marine Corps. He saw action during the Philippine Insurrection and the Boxer Rebellion in China. Zehringer was a native of Conshohocken, Pennsylvania and served with the Fourth U.S. Cavalry before becoming a member of the Force.

Some years later, Sgt. Marsh, who became a lieutenant, told Katherine Mayo that the Force owed a lot to Henry and Zehringer. *"As for the action itself, if we had to handle it again, we might handle it differently, but we were young then, all of us, with much to learn."*

As for Henry and Zehringer, *"They taught us to hold the honor of the Force dearer than life. They gave their own lives to do it, readily and gladly — and that's all any man can give."*

Over the next seventy years, more than seventy Pennsylvania State Policemen would die in the line of duty, and that doesn't count the many who died helping people during the Great Influenza epidemic after World War I.

... from the microfiche ...

No war or depression ever had as much as an impact on American morality (until TV) as did the revolution of the automobile. In 1900 there were about 8,000 cars registered. They were completely unreliable, owned by the rich and were mainly playthings. By 1917 there were nearly five million cars on the road that were pretty reliable, almost weather-tight and sold new for as little as $345.

"See them shuffling along
Hear their music and song
It's simply great, mate,
Waiting on the levee
Waiting for the Robert E. Lee"

... from the microfiche...

POLICE PAY PASSED

Harrisburg – June 1, 1911 – The State Police will earn more money. The General Assembly today passed an Act stating the members of the State Police Force shall be enlisted for a period of two years, each member of said State Police Force shall receive an increase in pay of five dollars a month during a second continuous enlistment, and an additional increase in pay of five dollars a month during a third continuous enlistment. The action by the lawmakers means that troopers serving more than two years on the Force will now be paid $730 a year and those serving more than four years continuously will earn $760 annually.

Associated Press

18.

LA MANO NERA

The Black Hand in Italy and Sicily had been around for a long time — since about 1750 — and lasted until about the 1920s when many of its practitioners made the transition into the Mafia. There were organized Black Hand societies in Spain that existed for hundreds of years to fight invaders and a Serbian Black Hand Society formed to establish dominance over the Balkans. The Italian/Sicilian Black Hand, however, was never really a society or a formal organization. It was primarily an extortion racket imported to America during the tidal wave of immigration of Italians and Sicilians at the turn of the century.

The racket affected mostly Italians wherever they gathered in large numbers, mainly in large cities from New York and Philadelphia to Chicago and San Francisco. But the smaller communities were just as much a target of these ruthless outlaws. Black Handers could be found pursuing their deadly game throughout the coal patches and steel towns of Pennsylvania with very little interference from the law up until the time of the Black Hussars. As noted, the attitude of the non-Italian population was, *"As long as they only kill each other, let them."*

The racket was uncomplicated — and deadly. A note would be sent to a victim threatening to kill him or a family member unless the recipient of the note handed over a specified amount of money. The notes were crudely written and often decorated with daggers dripping blood and other horrifying symbols. Instructions were included on how and where the cash should be paid. The signature of the sender was almost always a hand imprinted in heavy black ink, thus the sobriquet, La Mano Nera - The Black Hand.

Black Handers were usually anonymous, but some of them were so vicious, they used the ferocity of their reputation to enhance their proceeds. One of the most monstrous practitioners of this extortion racket was a New Yorker named Ignazio Saietta, known as the Wolf. Saietta strangled thirty people who refused to pay up. He then took their bodies to a livery stable he owned, chopped them up, burned what would burn and what would not burn he buried in his back yard. Saietta terrorized people for decades but was finally arrested for counterfeiting and sent to prison for thirty years.

The most famous victim of the Black Handers was the great Italian tenor Enrico Caruso. He paid off the Sicilian extortionists for years, reportedly one thousand dollars for every $10,000 he earned. Every time he appeared in New York, he received a Black Hand note politely informing him that if he did not pay the demanded extortion lye would be slipped into his tea or wine. Lt. Joseph Petrosino, a New York police officer, tracked down the Black Hander threatening Caruso, beat him up, dragged him to a ship and, ignoring a deportation proceeding, put him on board and said: *"If you return to this country, I will blow your brains out. If you bother Mr. Caruso again, anywhere on earth, I will find you and blow your brains out."*

Petrosino single handedly arrested hundreds of Black Handers including Saietta. The New York detective was murdered by the Mafia when he went to Palermo, Sicily, to identify Italian and Sicilian criminals he knew operated in New York and were wanted in their native countries. By identifying them he could have them deported from the United States.

In Pennsylvania, the Black Hand had been operating with seeming immunity until the State Police were called on to rid the state of this blight — at least in the rural area and coal towns. On February 16, 1907, the Philadelphia *North American* ran this dispatch from Wilkes-Barre: *"For the last five years the Black Hand Society has virtually had a free hand in the county. It has systematically levied tribute upon hundreds of Italians who paid considerable sums for protection from violence, and has committed numerous outrages upon others who refused to be blackmailed.*

The authorities have been almost helpless. Until the advent of the State Constabulary, the District Attorney's office had no force to make wholesale arrests, and besides, fear sealed the mouths of the victims. The fate of informers was well understood, for the society took pains to impress upon its victims that those who gave evidence against any member would suffer violent death.

On numerous occasions, frightened Italians have informed the police that they have received the usual threatening letters signed by the Black Hand, or have been personally threatened; but when told they would be required to appear as witnesses, they wilted; declared they could not identify anyone; that they had not even a suspicion of who the agents of the society were, and were glad to get away from the authorities and go back to their homes. Many have fled from the region to avoid the wrath of the society.

Even in flight there was no safety. A few months ago an Italian who refused to pay tribute fled with his family to Berwick, and there one morning was called to his door by three men and shot dead. Another who a year ago gave information against the organization was shot dead late at night at Pittston. Again there was no clue. A third was shot, beheaded, and his body was thrown into a mine-hole near Browntown ... there have been scores of outrages. Houses have been dynamited, men have been waylaid and wounded, women have been terrorized, houses have been fired upon or set on fire, but rarely have their been any arrests."

Wherever Italian immigrants congregated, the Black Hand soon made its ugly but powerful influence felt. As a rule, the victims were Italian merchants or tradesmen, or Italian laborers known to be thrifty and saving. The dreaded spell the Black Hand exerted in protecting its members and in defeating prosecutions of the State was present both inside and outside the courtroom. When witnesses appeared at a trial to testify against them, known Black Handers would enter the courtroom, stand at the rear, and draw their fingers across their throats, signals that meant all witnesses would be killed if they dared to testify. On other occasions, the signal of death was a red handkerchief drawn slowly from the breast coat pocket and wiped across the forehead, then dropped to the floor. The would-be witnesses always seemed to get the message and backed off from testifying.

The urgency of the situation called for immediate action. The district attorneys called on the State Police to gather evidence against this vicious, loosely knit group of murderers and thieves. In early February, 1907, at the request of the Luzerne County DA, several members of Troop "B" were detailed in plain clothes to investigate Black Hand activities in the area around Wilkes-Barre. On February 14th, a little over a week after receiving the request, Lt. George Lumb with a strong detachment of Troopers arrested 25 Black Handers in one raid. The trial was considered so important that the Federal Secret Service and the New York City Police Department sent observers who were in constant attendance in court. A connection was made at the trials linking Black Hand branches in Rochester, Buffalo and New York City with branches in Ohio and Pennsylvania towns.

The Black Handers arrested by the troopers near Wilkes-Barre were soon convicted and sentenced to prison. Then the State Police declared war upon the society throughout the Commonwealth. They attacked the Black Handers wherever they operated, first by going among them in plain clothes and gathering evidence, then swooping down on them and capturing whole bands at a time. On May 5, 1907, for instance, a "D" Troop force, operating on evidence gathered earlier, burst into a house in the coal mining town of Barnesboro in Cambria County where they knew a Black Hand meeting was taking place. They arrested 14 men, wiping out the entire local organization of the society. All 14 of the men were tried and convicted.

District Attorneys in other counties, encouraged by the action of the State Police, renewed their efforts to squash the Black Hand. Places such as Montgomery County were being overwhelmed by a Black Hand crime wave. Lawmen in this rural county just north of Philadelphia had to cope with incendiaries, dynamiting, kidnapping, white slavery, black-mail and extortion cases. Clearly something had to be done. The task demanded quick infiltration by detectives and then prompt and concerted action in force. Within a few weeks after moving into Montgomery County, the troopers had arrested every member of the Black Hand. The terrorists were terrorized. Over and over, in all parts of the State, the State Police used these tactics with unprecedented success. Occasionally the Black Hussars went openly into the areas infested by the Black Hand to clear them out without the preliminary use of disguises.

The reputation of the troopers was so strong by the summer of 1907 that members of the Black Hand fled at the sight of them, or at least hid, thus curtailing their operations. In Hillsville, a small town nearly on the Ohio border northwest of Pittsburgh, the district attorney of Lawrence County requested the assistance of the State Police to clean up the mostly Italian community that was being terrorized by members of the Black Hand. A sergeant and eight privates of Troop "D" were sent to Hillsville on August 8, 1907. They set up a State Police sub-station to assist the local authorities in wiping out the pernicious Society. Six weeks later, the troopers returned to their barracks in Punxatawney. In the short time they were in Hillsville, they had captured 23 members of the Black Hand, all of whom were subsequently convicted of their crimes and sentenced to long prison terms.

The change this action had on the town was described at the time by the *Pittsburgh Dispatch: "Hillsville no longer deserves the loathsome designation of 'Helltown.' Things have changed in the great limestone quarry settlement. Since the arrival of the State Police the Italians doff their hats as they canter by. Old residents sit on their porches these fine evenings and listen to the singing and playing of guitars ... saying it reminds them of Hillsville before the Black Hand was there. Then, when the day's work was done every man devoted himself to his home and family, and the newly arrived turned their thoughts to sunny Italy where a prospective bride was waiting to be brought to America. But when the terrible Black Hand agents reached the village they changed all that. Young men who were saving money to send back for a sweetheart soon learned to keep secret their ambitions. Songs in the summer evenings ended, and homes over which the Black Hand held the menacing stiletto or the smoking revolver never contained a light, for fear of attack by night. But all these terrors have now suddenly faded away; the arrest of the leaders and members of the Black Hand, have almost completely rid the community of the undesirable element, and the several thousand peace-loving Italians are assisting in the cleaning up in every way possible... "*

19.

ANOTHER TROOPER DIES

Private Timothy Kelleher was born in County Cork, Ireland in 1878. As a young man he fought in the Boer Army against the British in South Africa. At the end of the war, he came to the United States, joined the American Army and served with Troop D, Second Cavalry, and saw action in the Philippines. On December 15, 1905, he enlisted in the Pennsylvania State Police as one of the original Black Hussars.

When he was 29 years old, one year and nine months after joining the Force, Kelleher was on his way back to his "C" Troop barracks near Reading. He had been on leave and was unarmed. Walking along the road in civilian clothes, Kelleher was less than a half mile from the barracks when he heard a woman screaming. Rushing to her aide, he spotted the victim struggling with two men. As Kelleher battled with one of the assailants, the second man stabbed him in the back with a stiletto. The trooper, mortally wounded, fell to the ground. The woman had already escaped and the two men fled from the scene as Kelleher, bleeding heavily staggered a few steps toward the barracks, then collapsed and died alongside some railroad tracks. His fellow troopers found him there the following morning.

Every member of the Troop was ordered out to find his killer. Within three days they singled out and ran to earth Santo Pasquale, a cousin and confederate of one of the fugitives. He identified the killers of Kelleher — Salvatore Garito and Stefano Porcella — as two men with ties to the Black Hand Society. Through the efforts of Vincent Wadanoli, an Italian-speaking Trooper, it was learned that the fugitives were first sheltered by the local arm of the Black Hand and then fled to Warwick, New York.

Wadanoli and two other troopers, Privates William Booth and Alonzo Cady, all of them dressed in plain clothes, made their way by freight train to Warwick with Pasquale in tow. Upon their arrival in the upstate New York community, they heard that Garito and Porcella attached themselves to a railway labor gang that was on its way to Gray Court, some twelve miles away.

The three troopers went to the railroad officials, identified themselves, and asked that an engine be provided to take them to Gray Court. Their request was refused, so Booth and Cady rented horses at a livery stable and started off in pursuit of the train. Wadanoli stayed behind to guard Pasquale. As the two of them headed down the street toward a restaurant, Garito came around a corner and, seeing Pasquale, he broke into a smile and embraced him, ignoring the civilian clad trooper; but not for long. Wadanoli drew his revolver, told the fugitive to throw up his hands, handcuffed him, and marched him off to the local jail.

In the meantime, Booth and Cady caught up with the freight train outside of Gray Court. The train was stopped on a high trestle with the laborers still in the boxcar. Cady road his horse to the east side of the trestle while Booth dismounted on the west side. The two troopers then scaled the trestle at each end and, with revolvers drawn, advanced on the boxcar. Jumping into the car, Cady kept his gun on the gang of laborers while Booth handcuffed Porcella. Booth dragged his prisoner off the train, Cady followed, and they returned to their horses. While the troopers rode, they made Porcella walk back to Warwick, where they were delighted to learn that Wadanoli had captured Garito.

The three troopers, with their prisoners in irons, immediately boarded a train for Easton, Pennsylvania where they would change trains for Reading. Word of their successful manhunt had already reached their barracks and the Reading Chief of Police was informed about the capture of the two Black Hand members accused of murder. The news then spread throughout the city creating animosity from two different camps; a large crowd of Italians from Reading was gathering at the railroad station to attack the troopers and release the prisoners. At the same time, another large crowd of angry citizens was gathering to lynch the prisoners. The police chief called Easton to warn the troopers about a situation developing in the town and he urged them to somehow mask their entry into Reading. The chief was afraid the two groups might clash resulting in a bloody riot.

The problem was solved when Sgt. Cecil Wilhelm arrived at the railroad station with a large contingent of mounted Black Hussars ready to crush any outbreak of violence. When the train arrived in the city, there was some shouting between the citizens who wanted a lynching and the Italians who wanted to free the prisoners, but neither side had the stomach to go up against the State Troopers sitting their horses with batons drawn.

The two killers were jailed, tried and punished to the full extent of the law in spite of a determined effort by their lawyers to set them free. The three troopers, led by Private Wadanoli, had to travel on horseback and train through two states in order to find and capture the fugitives. It had taken just six days from the time Private Kelleher was murdered until the State Police had captured his killers and returned them to Pennsylvania from New York State to face justice.

... from the microfiche...

MAFIA AVENGED BY MYSTERIOUS CRIME

Night Watchman Saw Black Hand Victim Executed
Pittsburgh Address Clue May Lead to Murderers

New York February 8, 1910 – "Members of the Italian branch of the Detective Bureau are working hard to unravel a mysterious murder which took place early today and which the police see evidence of a plot to punish the man who revealed the secrets of an oath-bound society. A night watchman saw three men walking along 14th Street shortly before dawn. The other two men held the man in the middle by each shoulder. The watchman, James Johnson, said he followed the trio and when they got to First Avenue, they turned the corner. "When I looked around the corner, " Johnson said, "One of the men pulled a big revolver from his pocket and shot the man in the middle in the head. As he fell to the ground, the gunman fired again. Then the two men walked off."

The police came and took the body to the station house where they found a name and address in the victim's pocket that identified him as Antonio Gregoria of Pittsburgh. They also found cigars and candy and a vulgar verse in Italian.

The police are inclined to see some connection between the killing and the recent convictions of members of the Order of the Banana in Ohio. They say they have reason to believe he was decoyed to New York from Pittsburgh and was killed by the members of the Mafia or Black Hand"

" I'm going to Maxim's
Where fun and frolic beams
With all the girls I'll chatter

I'll laugh and kiss and flatter
Lolo, Dodo, Joujou,
Cloclo, Margot, Froufrou
I'm going to Maxim's
And you can go to..."

HOTEL MAN ELLSWORTH STATLER ADVERTISES:
A ROOM WITH A BATH FOR A DOLLAR AND A HALF

It was about 1 A.M., a lovely starlight night with no moon. The sea was calm with just a gentle heave as the boat dipped up and down in the swell, an ideal night except for the bitter cold. In the distance, the Titanic looked an enormous length, its great hulk outlined in black against the starry sky, every porthole and saloon blazing with light.

"Still all my song shall be
Nearer My God to Thee
Nearer to Thee"

The Titanic slowly tilted straight on end with the stern vertically upward and, as it did so, the lights in the cabins and saloons flickered for a moment, died out, came on again for a single flash and finally went out altogether. Meanwhile the machinery rattled through the vessel with a clatter and groaning that could be heard for miles. Then with a quiet, slanting dive...

———————————

As far as feasible, State Police Superintendent John Groome continued to honor every appeal for aid against the Black Hand. The result from the start was spectacular throughout the State. Every coal patch, small town and medium sized city was cleansed of the dread brought on by the secret criminal society. With mixed results, Philadelphia, Pittsburgh and the other major cities in the state used their own police forces to combat the organization that would soon change its ways and become the Mafia.

When Groome gave his summary of State Police activities for the year 1907, the Force had traveled, mostly on horseback, 332 thousand miles, visited 886 different towns or boroughs in 51 counties, and made 4,388 arrests for 54 different sorts of crimes. Of these arrests, more than three thousand had already resulted in conviction before the year was over and nearly a thousand more still awaited trials. With very few exceptions, all those arrests resulted in the criminals either going to jail or paying a stiff fine for lesser offenses.

As for the Black Hand, when Prohibition was made the law of the land in 1920, it vaulted petty thieves, flesh peddlers, bombers, extortionists and minor racketeers to the status of crime czars as they made bootlegging into a multimillion-dollar racket. The Pennsylvania State Police wiped out the Black Hand in the rural areas of the Keystone State, and the Volstead Act inadvertently brought relief to the Italian-Sicilian communities in the rest of America. The Black Handers quit the "petty" extortion racket to get deeply involved in bootlegging and crime syndicates. By the mid-1920s, the Black Hand was considered a relic of the criminal past.

PART V

A DIFFERENT BREED

20.

Physically, the original Black Hussars were above average in size and athletic adeptness in comparison to most men at the beginning of the Twentieth century. Yet only a very few of them were over six feet tall and those few were considered to be almost giants. Most of the troopers averaged five feet nine inches tall and weighed about 165 pounds. It would be unfair to physically liken them to the state police of today, just as it is unfair to compare today's athletes with those who lived seventy-five or one hundred years ago. After all, we are continually reminded that people today are bigger and stronger than they were in the past. Statistics and the facts prove that contemporary men and women are unquestionably bigger than their grandparents were — but stronger? It might be they only look stronger.

There is a program on television called <u>The World's Strongest Men</u>. These men are huge, six-feet-five and weigh-in at 260 to 300 pounds. They compete — for large sums of money, of course — to determine who is the strongest. One of several contests in which they display their strength is to lift a platform with several Las Vegas showgirls standing on top of it. Very impressive, until you see pictures of Eugene Sandow, a turn-of-the-century strongman, lifting a platform holding a piano and an eight-man band — playing music! And Sandow, although obviously well muscled, stood under six-feet tall and weighed less than two hundred pounds.

In the coal mines today, machines do almost all the work. In the past, the miners dug coal with picks and shovels. The scoops in those coal shovels were immense and held a lot of heavy coal. The miners shoveled tons of it ten hours a day, every day. They didn't live long, but while they lived, they were strong men.

Those who point to the sporting records that fall every year and attribute it to the "bigger, stronger athletes of today," are turning a blind eye to technology — the state-of-the-art shoes, the titanium and graphite in the computer designed golf clubs and tennis rackets, and the platoon and specialization systems of football and other sports.

THE BLACK HUSSARS

These are different times and comparison with the past is a futile exercise. The point is, unless one could put a John L. Sullivan in the ring with a modern boxer, a Bronco Nagurski on the football field with a 1990's lineman, who sits on the bench half of the game wrapped from head to toe in plastic protection, or see how far a Babe Ruth could hit the new, livelier baseballs, we have to accept that people in different eras can only be physically compared with other people from the same era.

The Black Hussars were unique for their time; extraordinary men who set a standard of performance and service for their organization that is unlikely to be surpassed or even matched, especially under modern political and social conditions. But, as tough and exceptional as they were, none of them were supermen. Indeed, they were quite human, saddled with the same faults and weaknesses mankind has faced since the dawn of civilization.

They did, however, have several things going for them as a group that modern police forces do not have. Foremost was their first Superintendent, Captain John C. Groome. He was the keystone of what was the finest police force in the world. Groome was in mind and action an officer and gentleman of the "old school." He also was tenacious of purpose, stern of judgment, prudent and practical, in love with discipline and law. He built the power of the State Police, demanded that it be free from political domination, and administered it with such wisdom and integrity that men would look to the Pennsylvania State Police as a rock of refuge through tempestuous decades. His grateful, early successors "canonized" him and, although it wasn't easy, those original Black Hussars who succeeded him managed for the most part to live up to his criterion of virtue and probity.

As for what Groome thought of his men, there was no doubt in anyone's mind. In a speech given on December 1, 1916, he said *"In a Force characterized by loyalty, intelligent devotion to duty, courage, and self-sacrifice, there is not one officer or seasoned Trooper in the entire Force who has not performed some act of duty that merits special commendation."* The keyword in that statement is "seasoned" trooper. Those who were not loyal and devoted to duty were quickly and unceremoniously discharged.

The man who first succeeded Groome was Captain George F. Lumb. While still Groome's assistant, Lumb once grabbed an influential politician by his coat lapels and threw him out of the Superintendent's office. The politician, a cabinet member, had tried to use his political stature in State Government to gain special treatment from the Force. He wanted a State Trooper assigned to him for what appeared to be personal services. Lumb said no to the request and the cabinet officer angrily threatened political retribution. That's when Lumb threw him out.

Another successor to Groome, Captain Lynn Adams, refused to ask a legendary State Senator to grant a college scholarship to the daughter of one of Adams' friends — the widow of a State Trooper. He told his friend that if he asked the politician for an accommodation, then the Senator might ask the State Police for a favor in return, and he did not want the Force to be put in that position. Adams instead offered to help the girl attend school out of his personal finances. Adams believed few circumstances were more detestable than owing a politician a favor, or more pathetic than a man who placed himself in such a position.

Groome, through policy, deed and example, set this apolitical course for the State Police at the very beginning when in 1905 he accepted the first superintendent's post on condition that the department should be kept free of politics. Using the military code as a guide, Groome issued General Orders which all members of the State Police had to obey. General Order Number 6 stated that "Any member of this Force known to have used outside influence (political pull) for the furtherance of his interests will be considered as acknowledging his incompetence and will be dropped from the service."

In a 1915 speech before the Colony Club of New York Groome said: *"And notwithstanding the fact that some of our leading politicians did try to control the appointments and to dictate the policy of the department during the first few years, I have always managed to keep the Force entirely free from politics and now it is at last recognized all through the State as an absolutely non-political body. In fact, I do not know and have never known the personal politics of any man on the Force. Neither of*

Governor Pennypacker's successors, Governor Stuart or Governor Tener, has ever interfered in any way with the management of the Force. "

This would change drastically by the 1950s as the old timers died off or were eased out of positions of rank and influence. Nevertheless, to this day most of the troopers continue their efforts to live up to the ideals Groome instilled in the first State Troopers who took to the field nearly a century ago.

Although the Black Hussars were not supermen, neither were they ordinary men. Lumb, Adams and the other successors of Groome, up until the retirement of Col. Cecil Wilhelm in 1955, were all members of the original Black Hussars when the State Police Force came into existence in 1905. With the exception of Groome, promotions came from the ranks and 95 percent of the troopers during the first ten years of the Force had served with honor in the U.S. Military during campaigns in Cuba, the Philippines and China. Like all of us, they surely were tempted from time to time by one or more of the Seven Deadly Sins.* But what made these men different from many of us is the self-discipline they exerted to resist temptation, coupled with their strong personalities.

There was one other reason why these men were a cut above the ordinary. Those who made it through the training and probation periods and survived for any length of time as Black Hussars, were the cream of the crop.

But making it through the first year as a Pennsylvania State Policeman was not easy. The attrition rate of the enlistees was horrendous. Out of an authorized strength of 232 men between 1905 and 1916, it at times seemed that as many men were being discharged as the number enlisting. In 1906

---

* Unlike the Ten Commandments given to Moses by God, the Seven Deadly Sins were authored by St. John Cassian and St. Gregory. These sins are pride, avarice, envy, wrath, lust, gluttony, and sloth. The Church also got around to adding acedia which means spiritual torpor, indifference. As America entered the 20th Century, the opportunity to relish all seven of the deadly sins was pretty much limited to the rich. The rest of the nation's citizens and immigrants, perhaps envious and wrathful at times, were otherwise too busy working long hours at low wages just to survive, leaving them little time or energy for sinning. For most of the last half of the century, however, plentiful supplies of money and free time have made the Seven Deadly Sins more widely available and, of course, when something is available, it is usually put to use.

there were 112 enlistments and 74 men discharged. In 1907, there were 109 enlistments and 99 men were discharged. In 1908, 68 enlistment's and 70 men discharged. Imagine the outcry today if sixty or ninety percent of the enlisted personnel of any police force was being mustered out every year because they fell short of the high standards set by the Superintendent. But those who met the standards set by Groome were the best of the best and it is what made the original Black Hussars such an elite force of men.

From its beginning through the 1950's, the Pennsylvania State Police Force was admired, copied by other states, and had a reputation for dedication, efficiency, fairness, and a determination to uphold law and order in the Commonwealth. During the first decade of their existence with fewer than 230 men on horseback this small band of troopers put down riots, tracked down and captured murderers, kidnappers, rapists, and thousands of other felons. They broke up the Black Hand in the area of their jurisdiction covering more than 40,000 square miles. Just as significantly, they built their cases in an extremely professional manner that resulted in an amazingly high conviction rate.

Not everyone, of course, was enamored with the new State Police Force. Aside from the criminal element, labor leaders were opposed to the formation of the Force even before Governor Pennypacker signed the Act that brought them into existence. And labor's opposition to the Black Hussars continued on the legislative and public opinion fronts for several decades.

In 1914, James Maurer, President of the Pennsylvania Federation of Labor, charged the State Police with "abuse of authority and employment of vicious methods." Governor Tener held public hearings to investigate the charges and the Black Hussars were exonerated. This didn't stop the labor leaders in their demands to abolish the State Police.

Failing in public hearings, they turned to the ballot box and called on their members to support only those candidates who would commit themselves to doing away with the "state constabulary," or seriously restrict its scope and powers. They also demanded the removal of Groome in favor of a political superintendent "more amenable to their influence," and demanded an amendment to the Act under which the department operates, prohibiting the "constabulary" from doing riot duty. All these efforts failed.

Ten years after Governor Tener's investigation, Governor Pinchot formed a Police Commission to investigate charges of State Police violence during the 1922 coal strike. A member of the Commission, labor leader John Guyer, wrote a pamphlet called "Pennsylvania's Cossacks." The pamphlet begins by referring to the earlier hearings instigated by Mauer. Guyer then summarizes the general perception of the Black Hussars noting that: *"For years, almost since its creation, the Pennsylvania State Police Force has been praised by state officials, employers of labor, and the press as one of the greatest organizations of policemen in the country. Every action in which its members have taken part has been given publicity of a favorable kind ... feats of horsemanship have been portrayed in story and pictures along with their work in capturing criminals and halting lawlessness. But in particular has the press sounded their praise when they appeared in the role of breakers of strikes."*

Guyer then went on to say: *"There is another side to this story ... It has never been completely written, save in the hearts of humble men and women whose heads and bodies have suffered from the clubs and hands of its vicious element whose actions have degraded and disgraced the state's power in the minds of the workers ... It is the story of cruel clubbing of men, and even women and children. Clubbings by irresponsibles who crept into the force for adventure. But frequently it was the deliberate action of brutal, drunken or depraved characters who have systematically used bloody force in executing orders of their superiors."*

These accusations are a bit hard to swallow. If there were any sadistic, vicious troopers as Guyer claimed and Maurer implied, they didn't last long and, in fact, never made it past Troop School or the probationary period. Weeding out the undesirables was one of the reasons there was such an incredibly high percentage of first-year troopers being dismissed from the Force.

It was Groome who designed the uniforms with a large number and Troop letter on the collar, which was not possible to remove without tearing the uniform. This was purposely done so that each trooper could easily be identified at a distance and was an innovation copied by the New York City and Philadelphia police forces. It was Groome who insisted that a policeman should also be a gentleman and to use no force beyond that necessary to maintain the law. And, perhaps most telling, while the state labor leaders were doing everything in their power to disband the State Police, or at least reduce their effectiveness, local union bosses constantly requested that Black Hussars be on hand at their annual picnics or at other big labor celebrations where crowds and drinking could lead to disorders or injuries. The Troop Captains always honored those requests by having one or two troopers present at labor events.

In its *Monthly Bulletin* published in August of 1914, the Pennsylvania Manufacturers Association (PMA), without mentioning the unions, replied to demands for abolition of the State Police by calling the Black Hussars *"... one of the greatest blessings the secluded farmers and the inadequately protected small towns of the interior have ever received from the government in Harrisburg and that the limitation of their sphere of usefulness would amount to a triumph for lawlessness throughout the Commonwealth."*

Aside from the protection the troopers offered, the PMA publication also brought up the subject of economics, making some interesting and telling points. In comparing the constabulary's limited manpower of 228 officers and men to its job of protecting 8 million people spread out over Pennsylvania's 45 thousand square miles, the report noted:
"Philadelphia has a police department of 3,987 men. Surely the great state of Pennsylvania, the only state in the Union which is without debt, can afford a (state) police force of at least 1,000 men!"

The PMA report then went on to note that during the nine years since the founding of the Force, the Pennsylvania National Guard was not called on once. Yet, without the Force, it would have been necessary for governors to have called out the Guard at least five times — at Chester in 1908, McKees Rocks in 1909, Philadelphia in 1910, South Bethlehem in 1910, and the anthracite fields in 1912. The last time the National Guard had been called on riot duty was at Hazelton in 1902. Nine thousand officers and men were pressed into service for eight weeks, costing the taxpayers one million dollars, not to mention the lost wages of the guardsmen who were kept away from their regular jobs for two months.

"This amount of money," the PMA report said, *"would be sufficient to support the State Police for three years, enabling them to accomplish the same results... ...and at the same time to give continuous service in the prevention and detection of crime of all kinds and the protection of life and property and womanhood in remote rural localities which otherwise would never see a uniformed officer of the law."*

When the automobile became a dominant force in American life, the Pennsylvania State Police formed a separate Highway Patrol Division in the early 1920's. It wasn't long until these police vehicles became known throughout the State as "Ghost Cars" because of their light gray coloring and the disconcerting habit they had of suddenly appearing behind errant motorists. In 1937, the Patrol was consolidated with the State Police and became known as the Pennsylvania Motor Police. Its authorized strength was 1,600 men. Then in 1943 the name of the organization was restored to the Pennsylvania State Police. But the Black Hussars continued to use their horses for controlling labor unrest until the mid-1930s.

Perhaps one of the finest hours in the history of the Pennsylvania State Police had nothing to do with crime or violence. It was 1918 and millions of young Americans marched off to help win World War One. Many of the Black Hussars were serving in the U.S. Armed Forces, including Superintendent Groome. General John "Black Jack" Pershing made Groome a Colonel and the head of all Military Police in the American Expeditionary Force. Captain George Lumb, Groome's assistant, took over temporary command of the Pennsylvania State Police while Groome was in France.

Despite the shortage of qualified men to fill the ranks of the Black Hussars, Lumb was determined to maintain the discipline and integrity of the Force and uphold the standards set by Groome. This resolve to preserve the honor and high ideals of the State Police, nurtured since its beginning, resulted in summary court trials for two troopers and an Acting Captain - leading to their dismissals from the Force. One trooper was charged with "abusing horses" and "failing to pay his debts." The other was charged with "fornication and bastardy" ... he had a child out of wedlock. The Captain was accused of "disloyal remarks" effecting "good order and police discipline." It's unlikely that any of these charges would result in even a suspension today.

It was also during this period that two more troopers were killed in the line of duty. Twenty-five year old Andrew Czap of Troop D in Butler, was shot and killed by four men when he was detailed to arrest them for a highway robbery in Indiana County. And just a month later, on May 31, 1918, twenty-one year old John Dargus of Troop A in Greensburg, was also shot from ambush in Ohio. He was detailed to pick up a fugitive murderer and was in the company of local Ohio police when gunned down. Both Czap and Dargus had been on the Force less than one year when they met their deaths. They were the ninth and tenth troopers to be killed in the line of duty.

The heroics of the Pennsylvania State Police during this period, however, were not confined to preserving law and order and dying from gunshot wounds, but rather from acts of mercy.

In the fall of 1918, the world was hit by a calamity seldom seen in the entire history of civilization. In a few short months, 21 million people died and more than one billion people — half of the world's population at the time — were affected by this catastrophe known as *The Plague of the Spanish Lady.*

"The Spanish Lady," Richard Collier wrote, *"inspired no songs, no legends, no work of art ... and to this day, no one can say with certainty where the disease began, where it ended, or even which virus was at fault."*

In the United States, influenza and pneumonia took at least a half million American lives — ten times as many as the Germans killed during the entire war. In Pennsylvania, the most severely affected state in the union, there were more than 350,000 cases of the flu and 36,000 people died. The Black Hussars put aside the work of law enforcement in favor of performing acts of compassion, disregarding the threat to their own health and lives. A report by Acting Superintendent Lumb notes that the *"... men worked day and night driving ambulances, taking doctors and nurses to the scenes of sickness and desolation in the foreign quarters of the mining regions, nursing the sick and caring for the destitute children of deceased parents."*

During the month of October, 1918, eight troopers died from the Spanish Flu while trying to save lives or bestow comfort and aid to those inflicted with this communicable and deadly epidemic. Incredibly, the courage and deaths of these men are not listed on department records as having been lost in the line of duty, an honor bestowed only on those who died violent deaths while on the job, such as by gun shots or stabbings. In fact, the troopers had to pay their own medical expenses. Moreover, the troopers had to take collections for the funeral expenses of men who were killed or died in the line of duty. And it gets worse. As Lumb noted, they *"... have been compelled even to pay the expenses of shipping home the bodies of their own comrades out of private funds."*

This shabby treatment of its law enforcement officers by the State was shameful, but in spite of it, the accomplishments of the Pennsylvania State Police in those early days is one of the finest chapters in American history. The reason behind their creation — rural crime, the economics of labor strife, or a combination of both — is murky and open for debate. The excellent result, however, is indisputable. Much has dramatically changed over this past century and, in many ways, for the better. With wages and home ownership high, and one or two cars in every garage, the economy, at least on the surface, has since World War Two been incredibly robust.

As the 20th century draws to a close, it would appear that in the long, often sordid history of man there was never a better time in the world than during the past fifty years in America. The crushing poverty borne by those in the early part of the century who worked in the sweatshops and steel mills, and the unbearable conditions suffered by the immigrant coal miners, is a thing of the past. Yet, crime is worse than ever, though now it is mostly in the urban areas instead of in isolated rural sections. Morality, honor, integrity and patriotism, a way of life for the Black Hussars and many people who lived in the first half of the century, are now laughed at outwardly by numerous Americans and surreptitiously by politicians, the press and the entertainment industry. In the past we were embarrassed in the presence of the crude and base, and today we are embarrassed in the presence of the noble.

As for the Pennsylvania State Police, it has, like all government agencies and bureaucracies, grown over the years to a size twenty times larger than the original Force although the physical size of the State remains the same and the population not quite a third larger than it was in the early part of the century. Today there are 4,200 State Troopers in Pennsylvania and the department employs an additional 1,200 civilians. Yet, today's State Police are rarely needed for strike and riot duty in the coal and steel regions which are not nearly as violent, frequent, and widespread as they were when labor first began to flex its muscles. In all fairness, the automobile presents problems that were not faced by the original Black Hussars. Sixty percent of the total on-duty time of the modern State Police Force is devoted to traffic and other public safety services, and forty percent of on-duty time is consumed by criminal investigations and administrative services.

It is interesting to note, however, that today's Pennsylvania State Police Force, as do almost all other major city and state police forces, has a Public Information Office with the main purpose of showing the force in a good light, and at no small cost. Yet, it's hard to find too many media stories singing the praises of today's cops. Usually, if the media pays any attention at all to the "thin blue line," it's often in a negative way.

By contrast, the Black Hussars had no public relations staff but, as Guyer wrote in his pamphlet, *Pennsylvania's Cossacks,* the force *"... has been praised by ... the press as one of the greatest organizations of policemen in the country. Every action in which its members have taken part has been given publicity of a favorable kind. "* The Black Hussars believed that actions spoke louder than words.

21.

THE FORCE TODAY

"We cannot capture the past and there is much in the past that we should not want to recapture. But neither is it irrelevant. If nothing else, history shows what can be achieved, even in the face of adversity. We have no excuse for achieving less in an era of greater material abundance ... "

Thomas Sowell - Imprimis

"It is winter, a cold day in Potter County, and a farmer stands screaming in his barn with his left arm caught in a piece of machinery. The farmer's wife is frantic. She is alone. Through the snowfall she sees the flashing lights of a Pennsylvania State Police car. A trooper jumps from the car and gingerly frees the man's arm. The farmer is losing blood. And with snow drifting, the ambulance might be delayed. There isn't a doctor for miles, so it's all up to the trooper. Cool, efficient, he rests the farmer in the rear of his car and heads off toward a hospital." A short time later, with the farmer hospitalized, the trooper is off on another assignment."

So begins the first of a seven part series by Associated Press writer Tom Baldwin describing the modern Pennsylvania State Police — or at least those in the 1970's as opposed to the original Black Hussars. Back then at the beginning of the century, the troopers patrolled on horseback, later in sedans and on motorcycles. But with the advent of turnpikes and the interstate highway system came specially equipped high-speed cruisers, radar and helicopters.

For nearly a century the Pennsylvania State Police has been the largest rural police department in the nation. *"The backbone of the department,"* said one trooper, *"is the guy riding alone down a country road."*

"Down in the cities," another trooper said, *"they don't even know what we look like. Out in the country, every head turns when we go past."*

Few troopers leave the force before they are eligible for pensions, mostly because the State Police have fashioned themselves an admirable reputation. They are considered by many laymen to be a cut above the average cop. They look more professional, are paid better, and their uniforms are more military-like, more impressive.

The men themselves (and now women) are mostly drawn from rural areas. They usually come from families where becoming a state trooper could be considered by some as a social step up. A lot of them are from the coal regions where they were raised amid the insecure and sometimes grimy future of going to work in the mines or with the railroads.

Most state policemen are tremendously proud of their job and of the heritage of the department. A lot of troopers who go to night school write term papers on the history of the Pennsylvania State Police, and a surprising number of troopers — including the older ones — can readily recite their oath of office which starts off with a ringing:

"*I am a Pennsylvania State Policeman, a soldier of the law...*"

In 1916, President Theodore Roosevelt was trying to encourage other states to form law enforcement agencies along the lines of the Black Hussars. Roosevelt wrote: *"The Pennsylvania State Police is a model of efficiency, a model of honesty, a model of absolute freedom from political contamination."*

A lot has changed since then. As Baldwin writes: *"The Pennsylvania State Police cannot escape politics. Be it a traffic ticket fix or simply the far-off rumblings of a Harrisburg shakeup, the trooper is keenly aware that the nature of his organization bares it to political forces."*

This is a far cry from the time when George Lumb threw a cabinet official out of his office, or Lynn Adams refused to ask a favor of a powerful State Senator knowing that the senator would want in return a favor from the State Police Force. It also was a long time ago that the Superintendents of the Force continued to serve in their positions as governor after governor would come and go.

"Sure we're political," says a veteran trooper from Westmoreland County. *"Every four years the new governor appoints a new commissioner, and every four years there is a shakeup of commanding officers.*

That's pure politics."

A state police criminal investigator in Philadelphia described at length how politics could corrupt the ranking officers, and how the influence of these officers subtly cripples the younger troopers.

"I was new on the job and my first assignment was traffic patrol on the Schuylkill Expressway," he said. *"There was a three-car accident, not a bad one; but there was a teen-age girl who caused it all. I wrote her up for reckless driving.*

"Two hours later I was back in the barracks taking a shower. Somebody shouted down that I had a phone call. It was Harrisburg. The deputy commissioner wanted to speak to me. I thought it was a joke. Why would the Harrisburg brass call a rookie trooper? I took the phone and he said he wanted to review the accident with me. He said he had the full report right in front of him, and he questioned my judgment. He asked if I really thought that the girl was at fault.

"I got the message. He was putting in the fix. It was subtle, but I was a rookie and here he was the deputy commissioner worrying about a simple little traffic accident. I let the girl's traffic citation 'dry up.' Later I checked on her and learned she was the daughter of a state representative.

"It was only two hours between the time of the accident and the phone call," the trooper said. *"That accident report didn't get to Harrisburg in no two hours. It had to be a phone call. Somebody called the deputy commissioner — and it wasn't me."*

One could argue that the trooper should have ignored his superior's esoteric "order." But in today's political climate it would almost certainly have been a kiss of death for his career. The persuasion the deputy superintendent used to intimidate the rookie would have gotten him kicked off the force under the command of a Groome, or Lumb, or Adams.

A trooper from Montgomery County put it this way: *"Every four years we get a kick in the teeth and then after the election we get a pat on the back. We're a political football, an easy target for anyone who wants to be governor of Pennsylvania. But we're more concerned with the job as we see it and do it than with who's upstairs in Harrisburg. We know the com-*

*missioners will change and they'll play the political game. But we're just
troopers and we'll do our jobs no matter who the boss is."*

Added to the "in-house" politics, there is the interference of the
federal government calling a lot of shots because no police department,
local or state, wants the D.C. money spigot to be turned off. Affirmative
Action and the law courts in the 1970s began ordering that more women
and minorities be promoted within the almost all white male department
regardless of their qualifications, and the "political correctness" of the 1990s
has put additional, subtle pressures on the men of the Force.

Yet, despite interference from various directions and sources, a vast
majority of the troopers in the field continue to live up to the standards of
the original Black Hussars. Not just in Pennsylvania, but in most states
throughout the nation.

The first Pennsylvania State Policemen, almost to a man, came
onto the Force after serving under fire in the military. They were physically fit to start with and then underwent additional training with weapons,
horses, and classroom sessions to learn the law and how to deport themselves with the public. The training for state troopers today is just as exten-
sive if not more so. A majority of troopers who make it through the acad-
emies in their respective states, (in spite of "special" treatment for some)
are the elite of law enforcement.

One thing hasn't changed since the tenure of Superintendent
Groome. The Pennsylvania State Police — as well as those in other states
— are taught to be gentlemen. It's always, *"Yes, sir,"* and *"No, sir,"* and
*"Sir, I'd like to inform you that you are under arrest. Please have a seat in
the rear of my car."*

Perhaps the biggest difference between the state police forces of
today and those of fifty or seventy-five years ago is contending with the
mores of an affluent society that at times seems to have gone completely
berserk — children from "good" families gunning down their classmates,
pornography readily available to anyone who has a television set or is on
the internet, overcrowded courtrooms as the same criminals go through
them like a revolving door, convicted murderers who are back on the streets

killing again within a few years of first being locked up — if they go to jail at all; rapists, serial killers, drive-by shootings at schools and in neighborhoods. The list of crimes is endless, and the volume of crime is like the national debt — astronomical.

From a television news program — Spring, 1998
Between 1994 and 1997, the State of New York spent $3 million to provide medical treatment and all the drugs necessary for prisoners who wanted to have sex changes. During this period, 87 prisoners used these services. Some of those prisoners committed crimes just to get in jail and have the taxpayers foot the bill for the very costly process of changing their sex. One wag asked, "After they become women, do they stay in the same jails, making them coed prisons?"

In 1968, Richard Speck killed eight nurses in their Chicago dormitory. Armed with a revolver, Speck tied up the nurses and one by one, dragged them into an adjoining room where he either stabbed them to death or strangled them. One of the nurses he had tied up managed to slide under a bed and hide. When Speck finished with his bloody orgy, he had forgotten that one nurse who remained hidden until he left the dorm. Within three days, Chicago police had Speck in custody and a short time later he was put on trial. The evidence against him was overwhelming — fingerprints, blood samples, clothing. But most damming of all was the testimony of the surviving nurse who, at one point in the trial, left the witness box, walked directly up to Speck, pointed her finger at him and said he was the killer. Speck was convicted of the brutal murders of the eight nurses and was sent to prison where he died twenty-five years later from a heart attack — after doctors spent four hours trying to save his life.

This wasn't the last of Speck, however. He left behind a "memorial" as macabre as the slaughter of the nurses. *"If they knew how much fun I was having in here, they'd turn me loose. I can get more drugs, money and sex in here than I could ever get on the outside."*

That comment was made by Speck on videotape that he and other prisoners made. It was shown in June, 1998 on a television program called *Investigative Reports*. The prisoners not only had access to video cameras, but also to what seemed like an unlimited supply of drugs and money. They made a pornographic movie in the prison and Speck was the featured "star." He apparently had some sort of sex transformation. His naked breasts seen on the TV show were those of a well-endowed woman. His "lover" interviewed him and Speck, laughing, described how he killed the nurses. When asked if he had any remorse, he said *"Not for a moment."*

Drugs, sex, money, TVs, computers and weight rooms. Guards that are fearful, politicians and prison officials afraid of offending vociferous constituencies and the news media, all do nothing to correct a system that has reached a point of insanity. During the first half of this century, prisons were places of punishment meted out by society. Today the punishment is meted out by the inmates while society tries to provide the prisoners with every amenity short of complete freedom, even bizarre, expensive medical treatments. As an extension of the prison system, the police are faced with the same political and media pressures. The result has been that some of those in the hierarchies of law agencies — federal, state and local — act like they are more concerned about promotion, favorable attention from the news media, and holding on to their positions, than upholding the law and maintaining order.

On a warm, sunny afternoon in Seattle during the summer of 1997, a mentally disturbed man began to wave a machete at people in one of the city's busiest downtown areas. Police arrived and tried to convince the man to put down the machete. He threatened the police who were ordered not to harm the man. Within a short time, a large section of the city was blocked off, traffic was re-routed and snarled, and commuters trying to get home from work were unable to take their buses back to the suburbs. For six, long hours the man walked back and forth in front of a building, waving his machete at scores of policemen who were not allowed to lift a finger to subdue the fellow.

165

Eventually, the fire department arrived and knocked the man off his feet with a powerful spray of water. He was then taken into custody and sent to an institution. The police were praised for not hurting the man. They also were condemned for allowing him to shut down part of the city at considerable cost to businesses, the taxpayers (a large force of policemen and firemen eventually became involved in subduing the man) and for the great inconvenience to thousands of working people trying to get home.

Recall the story of the "insane" man who in 1914 barricaded himself in his house and with a large butcher knife, threatened to kill anyone who came near him. Two Black Hussars went into the dark house and, while one put a flashlight on the man, the other trooper shot the knife from the man's hand. "It was then possible," said the "A" Troop report, "to close with him without any particular injury to officers or the prisoner." They did what they felt needed to be done and the entire incident was over a few minutes after their arrival on the scene.

The police officers on the scene of the machete-waving man in downtown Seattle, may very well have wanted to take decisive action against the man and quickly end the incident instead of standing around waiting for a decision to come down the chain of command at police headquarters. While the cops stood around and waited for the chief and politicians to decide what to do with the machete-waving man, a large crowd was shouting suggestions (or derision), and the news media was having a field day. All the cops wanted to do was overpower the man and haul him away. But their orders from above prevented quick, forceful action. Doing the same thing today that the state troopers did eighty-five years ago, would most likely result in suspension, a board of inquiry, and possibly criminal charges against the police, depending on the public defender of the insane man.

The diffident response by many of today's law enforcement personnel to situations of crisis is more often than not brought about by orders from above and the fear of what the media would do if something went wrong during a course of action. Cops today work under terrific restraints and pressure, but still manage to protect society.

When the political climate, conduct and morality of contemporary society are taken into consideration, the Black Hussars would be proud of many of the men and women in the ranks of today's State Police throughout the nation. Teddy Roosevelt's wish to see all states follow Pennsylvania's lead has been fulfilled. And, as a consummate politician himself, he surely must have foreseen with sadness the political games that would be played when the original commanders of the Black Hussars died off and a bureaucracy inserted itself into the top echelons of the Force. But it is highly doubtful that he or anyone else could foresee such a rapid decline in American social values since the 1960's.

Robert Bidinotto, a Staff Writer for Reader's Digest and a lecturer for the Foundation for Economic Education, summed up modern mores exquisitely in an article he wrote a few years ago about cultural pollution. In part, he said:

"There actually was a time in this nation's not so distant past when most kids wouldn't use foul language around the opposite sex (not to mention at adults), and when those few who did would get their faces slapped. A time when no one would have dared ask the President of the United States what kind of underwear he wore, and when no President would have dignified such a question with an answer.

It was a time when students referred to teachers by their surnames, teachers refused to pass kids who hadn't met minimum standards of achievement, high school graduates could read job applications, and schools issued more books than condoms. A time when unmarried girls actually felt ashamed to get pregnant and when unemployed men actually felt ashamed to apply for welfare. When derelicts didn't use sidewalks or celebrities the airwaves, as public latrines.

During the past four decades, standards of personal taste, language, behavior, dress, and manners have plunged to loathsome levels. Today we are awash in a cultural tsunami of vulgarity and incivility. From the street corner to the school classroom from the movies to MTV, belligerent faces stare back at us in defiant challenge to all that is decent and good, virtuous and valuable... we are simultaneously revolted and incredulous ...wondering from what buried cesspool of our national life such pollution

167

has oozed forth." '

Superintendent Groome and his men were not saddled with the burden of an insolent public, parents afraid of their children, teachers in fear of their students, citizens who ignored or twisted the laws to their own ends. This, however, is the kind of society faced by the troopers of today, coupled — in many instances — with laws and a bureaucracy and hierarchy dedicated to pleasing political correctness at the expense of honor and integrity.

The Black Hussars were quite often under tremendous physical pressure and stress from the duties they had to perform in keeping the peace of the State. But, as long as they obeyed the rules and did their duty, they never had to worry or even think about the machinations of the politicians in the State Capital.

What is amazing about the Force today — and all State Police forces throughout the nation — is that so many of the troopers and officers perform so admirably in the face of internal and external pressures brought to bear on them by political leaders, special interest groups and, in some cases, their own top commanders.

Despite current laws, federal and state regulations, a generally antagonistic news media, and politicians concerned first and foremost with getting re-elected — in spite of all these handicaps forced on the modern police force, the Black Hussars of nearly a century ago could only be satisfied with the legacy of their efforts and would undoubtedly be honored to serve with the majority of today's elite troopers.

SOURCES

I. Primary Sources

Conti, Phillip M. Lt. Col. Penna. State Police, (Ret.)
THE PENNSYLVANIA STATE POLICE Stackpole Books
Harrisburg, PA 1976

Mayo, Katherine, JUSTICE *TO ALL*   Putnam
New York, 1917

II. Secondary Sources

Dos Passos, John, THE *42ND PARALLEL (Part of the USA Trilogy)*
Washington Square Press
New York 1961 - originally published in 1930 by Houghton Mifflin
(permission to use material granted by Lucy Dos Passos Coggin)

Poliniak, Louis, *WHEN COAL WAS KING* Applied Arts Publishers
Lebanon, PA 1977

Sifakis, Carl, ENCYCLOPEDIA *OF AMERICAN CRIME*
Smithmark Publishers, Inc.
New York, 1992

Baldwin, Tom, SOLDIERS *OF THE LAW*
Associated Press series on the Penna. State Police which appeared in the
Johnstown (PA) Tribune Democrat
November 1974

Bimba, *THE MOLLY MAGUIRES* International Publications, Inc. New
York, 1932

Gambino, Richard, BLOOD OF MY SOUL, Doubleday,
Garden City, NY 1974

Collier, Richard, PLAGUE OF THE SPANISH LADY,
Athenaeum Publishers,
New York, 1974

Maurer, James, THE AMERICAN COSSACK,
Pennsylvania Federation of Labor,
Reading, Pa 1915

Bidinotto, Robert, CULTURAL POLLUTION,

Foundation for Economic Education Magazine,
Irvington-on-Hudson, NY March, 1995

Other sources include mainly the Cambria County Library's
Pennsylvania Room and the library's microfiche files, which provided
much of the material about the state and the world during the early
decades of the 20th century.

In addition, the Windber Area Museum, Inc., Windber, Pennsylvania, and The Texas Department of Public Safety, Austin, Texas were
helpful in my research.

Index

173